D0939118

Peter Sellers

A Celebration

Acknowledgements
This book would not have been possible without the tireless help of countless people. In particular, I would like to thank Glenn Mitchell, whose encyclopaedic archivism remains difficult to beat, Dave Sheppard, a photographic scholar unsurpassed, Michael Pointon, Marcus Hearn, Chris Smith of The Goon Show Preservation Society and Joe McGrath.

Also Roy Hudd, Sir Alec Guinness, Simon Callow, Rod Morgan, Jo Leonard, Kevin Davies, Derek Webster, Danni Webster, Cassie Swinfield, Patrick Garland, Brian Blessed, Hildegard and Rosalind and Nicola, Mum and Midge...

I would like to pay special thanks to Rod Green, whose editorial duties have gone above and beyond the call of duty on this particular volume, as is the case with Lorna Russell, and also Geoff Tibballs, without whom this book would not be what it is...

In addition to the author's acknowledgements, the publishers would like to thank Spike Milligan, Eric Sykes, Graham Stark, Burt Kwouk, Mark Eden, Dennis Selinger, Roy Boulting and Maurice Denham for their very special contributions to this book, and they are also hugely grateful to Maxine Ventham for her invaluable help throughout the editorial process.

First published in 1997 by
Virgin Books
an imprint of Virgin Publishing Ltd
332 Ladbroke Grove
London W10 5AH

Inside photographs courtesy of Adrian Rigelsford and Hulton Getty.

A catalogue record for this book is available from the British Library.

ISBN 1 85227 623 1

Designed by Design 23, London
Printed by Butler & Tanner

Peter Sellers

A Celebration

Virgin

Contents

Foreword by Spike Milligan

Peter Sellers was a friend. I met him in the bar of the Hackney Empire where I went to see Harry Secombe's famous shaving act. Harry talked so fast he sounded like a visiting Polish comic.

As I didn't drive I had Sellers as my personal driver. He was obsessed with cars. Just for the pleasure of it he would drive into the countryside, including driving into a brook one day and I was collared to wash the mud off the car.

Back at his parents' flat we experimented with his new-fangled tape recorder. Our favourite trick was to record the voices at slow speed then play them back fast. We became fast friends and I would sleep on the floor on a pneumatic mattress which I would blow up only to find by morning it had a leak and I was sleeping on the stone floor.

Peter had a toe-hold with the BBC. He introduced me to a 'rebel' producer, Pat Dixon, who had our sense of humour and he commissioned me to write a trial script. Peter suggested some voices and it was recorded and was well received. The others in the show were Michael Bentine and Harry Secombe. That was the start of *The Goon Show*.

I was living opposite Sellers and at 3 o'clock one morning there was a knock on my door. When I opened it Sellers was standing there naked except for a Trilby hat, socks and shoes. 'Good morning! Do you know a good tailor?' he asked. I got my own back by sending him a telegram the next day saying 'Ignore first telegram'.

Alas, he was obsessed with beautiful women. He had an affair with Sophia Loren and then seemed to lose his way. He was now a big star. He then went mad over Britt Eckland, and next came Lynne. Then the clock stopped.

I suppose the days when he was happiest was during the *Goon Shows*. He once said to me that he had never exceeded that level of happiness.

His death to me was the loss of a genuine friend. I will never forget his funeral. In the middle of the service the loudspeakers blared out 'In The Mood', a tune he hated.

Peter, I miss you.

The Goons with programme-announcer Wallace Greenslade.

Chapter 1

Inspector Clouseau and the Ideal Gnome Exhibition

'There's an advantage to being associated with comedy . . . because people think that you're being funny . . .'
Peter Sellers interview, *The Daily Sketch*, 1967

Handy Gardening Hints was a bi-weekly programme that was broadcast on one of the English-speaking radio stations in Calcutta for many years. During the late 1960s, when some of the more bombastic colonial types were still in residence, a retired general was once the show's guest speaker, and proceeded to give a rather patronising lecture on how it was only the British who knew how to grow rhododendron bushes with a sense of panache.

Midway through the transmission, a phone call was received from an Indian gentleman who wanted to ask the general for some tips on how to control a bonfire in a residential garden. The caller was connected through to the studio and started to chat on air. When he asked if a smoking turban was a sign that he was standing too close to the flames, the show's presenter began to sense that there was something that was not quite right, and asked the caller for his name. It was Singhiz Thingz.

Peter Sellers was in India at the time. The two events are not entirely unrelated. You could almost put a casebook of evidence together to prove that Sellers had a rather bizarre sense of humour, and it certainly seems to have been at work throughout the course of his career.

In the mid-1950s, when *The Goon Show* was both a national institution and pastime, Sellers was practically living next door to the show's main creative force, Spike Milligan. Once, in the middle of the night, Milligan awoke from a deep sleep and realised that someone was hammering on his front door. After checking a clock to see that it was about half-past three in the morning, he headed downstairs to investigate.

After opening the door, Milligan found himself confronted by a man wearing nothing more than a bowler hat, who was calmly standing on his doorstep and leaning against a rolled-up umbrella. It was Sellers, but before Milligan could even utter a single vowel, he was asked if he knew of any good tailors in the area that he could recommend.

It seems that Milligan was also one of a number of Sellers' close friends who fell victim to one of his favourite practical jokes, and once again, it involved people being roused from their slumber. It went something like this: Sellers would turn up at his target's house, and it would be well past midnight. A plea would be given, asking for help to locate the source of a strange rattling noise coming from the rear end of a car that he'd just purchased.

After examining every possible angle of the exterior of the vehicle, Sellers would scratch his head and announce that there was only one thing for it - the 'friend' would have to climb inside the car's boot, armed with a torch and a piece of chalk, and mark the closest spot they could find to the sound as Sellers drove down the road with them on board.

Bouncing up and down the kerbs of a suburban road would offer no evidence of a single squeak, but inflict plenty of bruises on the driver's hidden passenger. Sellers would then suggest that it probably only rattled at speed before heading for a motorway, despite the loud protests from the boot. After a hair-raising journey, the victim would be delivered back to the safety of his home and more head scratching would ensue, with Sellers concluding that the extra weight in the rear must have sorted the problem while they were out driving. It was an admirably elaborate wind-up.

In Milligan's case, the trick backfired because Sellers was pulled over by the police when they saw the erratic route he was taking along a kerbside. The driver smiled his most sincere smile, but it didn't stop the investigating constable from hearing the loud banging coming from the boot. When the lid flipped open, he shone his torch on Milligan, recognising him instantly, and said, 'Oh, it's you,' and then let him go, obviously not wanting to interrupt the goonery that was underway. Or was it simply that he couldn't figure out how the hell to fill out a report form and convincingly explain what was going on?

Sellers' antics were not just confined to his leisure time. Some of the more infamous incidents attributed to him occurred while he was filming, and they vary from tales of Peter simply fluffing his lines to rather more intriguing stories. The Pink Panther films alone offer a huge catalogue of behind-the-scenes mishaps to choose from.

Mastering how to use certain props was a skill that eluded Sellers on the odd occasion, and when it came to completing one of the scenes for *A Shot in the Dark*, you could hardly blame him for getting into what could best be described as a bit of a state. As far back as the early 1900s, W.C. Fields was causing a sensation whenever he performed his pool table routine on stage, which involved him

Sellers and George Sanders filming a particularly demanding scene in *A Shot in the Dark*.

trying to play the game with a series of cues that were curved at impossible angles. So, the notion of letting a certain Inspector Clouseau loose with one of the self-same cues seemed like a brilliant idea, but . . .

The scene involved George Sanders (as Monsieur Ballon) inviting Clouseau to join him for a game of billiards. One of his first camera angles to be set up was a close-up on Sellers as he tried to hit a ball with the malformed cue. In principle, this was a simple enough thing to try to commit to celluloid, but in its execution, three cues were snapped and the ball was sent into orbit in a variety of directions. By the twentieth take, Sellers was in hysterics because he physically could not bring himself to miss the ball as he was meant to do. A separate shot where Ballon gets his cue caught up with the inspector's was set up instead.

On the first take the actors could not

escape from the knot they got themselves tied into, on the second Sanders got hit on the nose by Sellers' elbow, and by the third attempt they managed to get out of the tangle and then both promptly started to giggle. The same routine was tried over and over again, and Sellers was finally reduced to tears of laughter as he found that he could no longer say Ballon properly. The surname of Sanders' character kept coming out as Balloon and Baboon.

Similar strange mispronunciations of certain words brought take after take to a grinding halt on other films in the series. Sir Charles Litten, the notorious Phantom, became 'Sir Charles Phantom' and 'the notorious Litten', and Clouseau himself once confessed to being 'a renowned trouble shitter' instead of 'shooter'. Simple sound effects could also cause problems, and on *Revenge of the Pink Panther* it was perhaps slightly naive to expect the filming to go smoothly when one of the sequences involved a character audibly breaking wind in a crowded lift.

The set-up was as follows: Clouseau was heavily disguised and padded out to Brandoesque proportions as a Mafia don called Scallini, and in a scene lasting no longer than fifteen seconds on screen, he is seen being escorted down to the lobby of a vast hotel in its main elevator. The sound effect for the said flatulence was due to be added during post-production, so the actors needed a cue in order to be able to react to the noise at the right moment. That's when things began to go wrong.

Director Blake Edwards volunteered to cue in Sellers and the others when the appropriate moment arrived - and that's when he blew what was probably the fruitiest raspberry that's ever been heard. Sellers was the first one to hit the floor as he howled with laughter, and the other three cast members slowly slid down the walls of the lift to join him. Edwards called for a second take to be set up, but it was optimistic of him to think that the end was in sight.

For the next 25 takes he varied the pitch, tone and clarity of each successive raspberry, but the actors still corpsed with alarming regularity, and it was always Sellers who

Sellers and director Blake Edwards take a break from filming.

was the first to go. Edwards then decided to use the word 'Now' as an alternative cue, but this simply made matters worse and a make-up man had to be called in to repair the damage that the laughter was inflicting on Sellers' delicate prosthetics. In the end, after another five takes, a lunch break was called.

When the four actors returned, they had another go. This time they actually got beyond the cue word, but when somebody's lunch made an unexpected return appearance, a belch suddenly echoed around the set. Sellers slowly turned to face the wall behind him and started to bang his head against it, before slowly sliding down to the ground once again in a renewed fit of giggles.

It's that final take that can be seen in the finished movie, with the burp simply erased from the soundtrack, although Sellers can still be seen turning towards the rear wall as he tries to hold back the laughter.

Another seemingly impossible-to-complete scene was staged on the Panther film that immediately preceded *Revenge – The Pink Panther Strikes Again.*

The moment in question involves Clouseau's arrival at a hotel, where he's confronted by a near incomprehensible, partially deaf and anciently decrepit receptionist. The part was being played by Graham Stark, and his old-age make-up was only brought into use during a remount of the sequence, because an earlier attempt had resulted in total chaos. With Edwards directing once again, his original idea was to have Stark looking like Adolf Hitler, but when they tried to film it, Sellers simply couldn't keep a straight face and that caused Stark to have hysterics as well.

One of the props that had been given to Stark to use in the reworked version of the scene was a massive pipe, and when he began protesting about the fact that he no longer smoked, he was quickly reassured that its bowl had been loaded with a herbal tobacco substitute. Filming got underway and Stark promptly began to feel rather light-headed as he puffed away on the stuff, and as the smoke reached Sellers, his all-too-familiar giggling fits suddenly started.

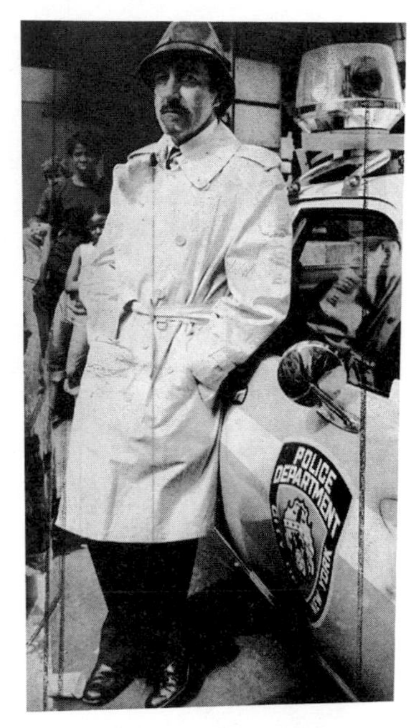

Inspector Clouseau was made an honourary detective of the New York City Police Department.

The fumes were soon being inhaled by Edwards and the rest of the film crew as well, and just like the two actors, they began to start laughing as nearly every take crumbled before their eyes. Someone had planted the idea in the head of one of the props team to fill Stark's pipe with pot, and to make sure that there was enough for the intoxicating smell to hit everybody on the set.

Sellers at 'The Ideal Gnome Exhibition'.

It never became apparent as to exactly who it was who dreamt up the scheme - and the film crew had a bad enough time trying to remember who they were by the end of that day. However, you don't have to be Agatha Christie to hazard a shrewd guess over who the culprit might have been. Sellers was sometimes on the receiving end of jokes as well, and the most peculiar example of this happened while he was making *Hoffman* during the winter of 1969.

Yul Brynner had lent Sellers a luxurious trailer to use while he was out shooting at Elstree Film Studios, and one morning he found that somebody had laid out a strip of artificial turf in front of its doorway. When he asked about this, nobody knew anything about it, but all agreed that it made it look more homely. This point was stretched a bit further during the following day, when Sellers arrived at work and found that a rope fence had been erected around the turf, and during the lunch hour Hoffman's producer, Ben Arbeid, presented the actor with a garden gnome to complete the image that had been created. And that was just the start of it . . .

Every morning, something new mysteriously appeared on the grass - stone owls, wooden penguins, model windmills and plaster rabbits - but it was generally the gnome population that seemed to be on the increase. The studio's special effects unit even joined in and created a monstrous three foot high model of a pair of the creatures, with one gnome trying to push the second off a giant toadstool. There was even a gnome version of Inspector Clouseau that turned up, complete with a raincoat and moustache, sitting on a mushroom with a broken fishing rod.

These strange donations along the front of Sellers' temporary accommodation were all made anonymously by the Hoffman production team, and he even took part himself and made a hand-painted sign to hang on the front of the rope fencing, which read 'Welcome To The Ideal Gnome Exhibition 1969'. As he left the trailer each night when filming had finished for the day, Sellers always made a point of affectionately patting several of the gnomes on the head to say goodnight to them.

Stories like this tend to suggest that working with Peter Sellers must have been a strange experience. Many well-known actors have admitted that even if they had the most glorious stage and cinematic triumphs to their credit, when people realised that they'd appeared in a film with Sellers, the whole direction of the conversation would suddenly change course and concentrate solely on what he was like to work with.

Sellers died in July 1980, and if anything, the public's fascination with the man both on and off screen has increased dramatically since that time. Numerous documentaries have been made, hundreds of thousands of words have been written, and retrospective seasons of his films have been put together, and the purpose behind all of them has always been the same - to try to figure out exactly what it was that made Sellers tick.

Whether it's Clouseau, Fred Kite, Bluebottle or Major Bloodnok, it seems that everybody can name at least one creation of his or quote a line of Sellers dialogue. But where did it all begin? What's the background behind the man who left such an indelible mark on the history of comedy? Well, you have to go back quite a long way to find the roots of this particular life story . . .

Hoffman co-starred Sinead Cusack and was directed by Bryan Forbes.

Graham Stark

Graham Stark worked with Sellers on countless projects from the Goons through to the Pink Panther films, in which he played Clouseau's side-kick, Hercule.

When I think of Peter, I think LAC Sellers. (Leading Aircraftsman). The first time I met him I was walking out of what is now the London School of Economics but was then taken over by the Air Ministry, and there was this rather plump-looking airman breathing on the bonnet of a car, polishing it. I was amazed: not only did an airman have a car - this was wartime - but that car was very large and American. He ignored the fact that I happened to have three stripes and said, 'Only does 22 to the gallon but a bit of class!' Hysterical!

We wandered off and had a cup of tea together. He asked, 'Where do you live?' and I told him I lived in the Service Club. He couldn't believe it and he said, 'You can't live there, come on.' We jumped into the car, collected my gear and off we went, up to North Finchley. He lived in the top flat with his mum and dad and delivered this great dramatic speech. It was wonderful, terribly over the top: 'Look at this poor lad. He's got nowhere to live...' I stayed there until I went away to work. That was very typical of Peter. It was instant friendship and it never changed.

I have so many fond memories of him. We lived in our own private world of comedy and fantasy - those childish, idiotic voices. Peter was a phenomenal mimic. He was the only the man I've ever known who could completely change his voice. He'd talk on the telephone to me and I wouldn't know it was him. It was extraordinary.

Bloodnok was a source of great joy to us. He'd

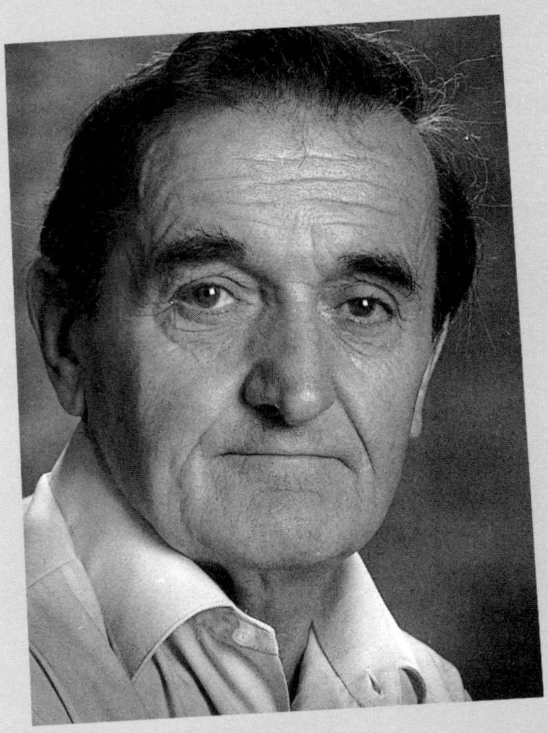

The ubiquitous face of Graham Stark.

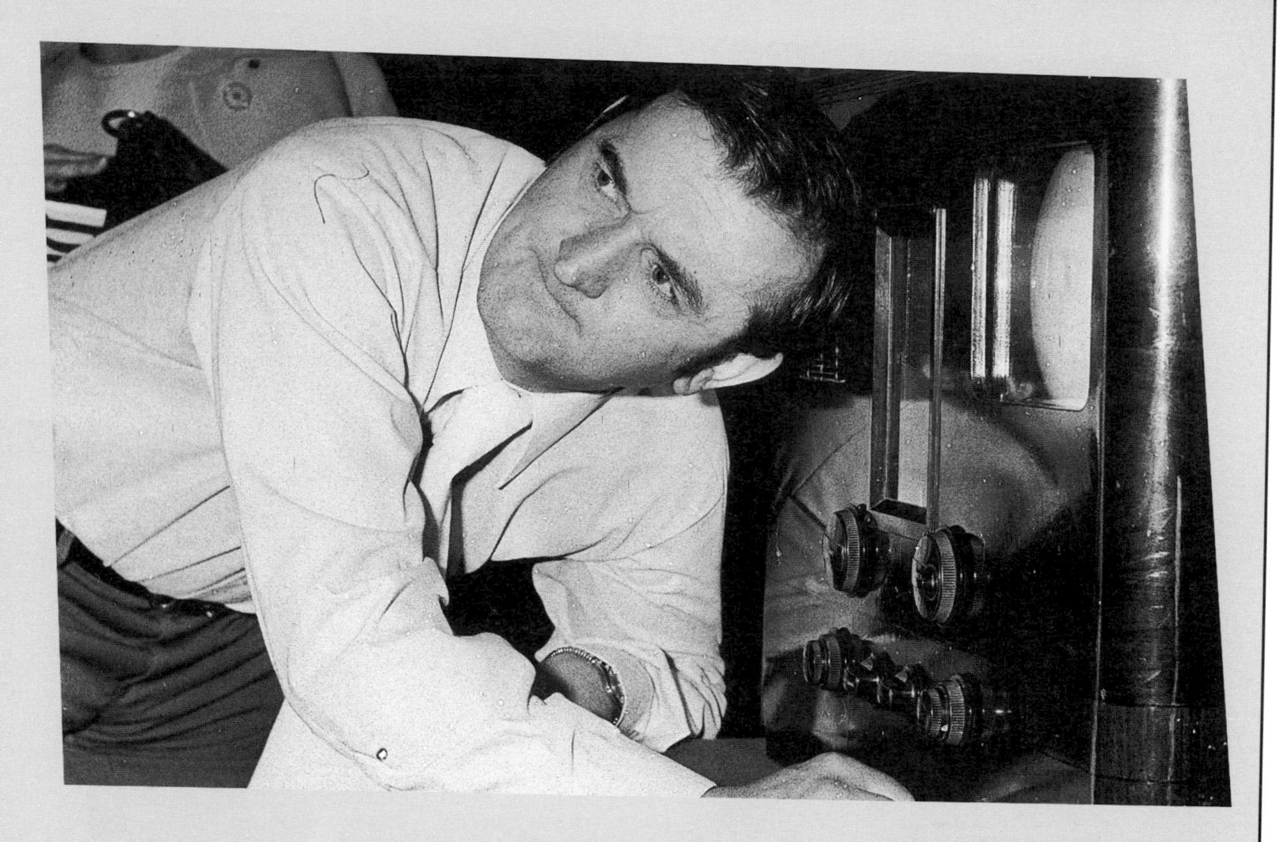

Popular star in both mediums, Graham tunes into an early combined TV and Radio set.

phone me up as Bloodnok and say 'Guess what?' And it could be anything from, 'I have a new Bentley covered in gold paint' to, 'I'm going to do this film in Italy with an unknown director called Blake Edwards and guess how much they're paying me?' He wasn't materialistic but he loved things. He was a schoolboy in many ways.

In my opinion, Peter's best ad-lib was in *The Wrong Box* as Dr Pratt. It was a marvellous performance; very sad and lugubrious. He used one of the cats as a blotting pad, which was very funny, but then suddenly, at the end of the scene he leant forward, looked terribly sad, looked straight at this cat and said, 'It's not good for you.' It was a wonderful non-sequitur ad-lib and I love that line. I once met Claudette Colbert and we spent our entire time talking about Dr Pratt and the cats.

Peter was always the first to start giggling! There were so many giggling scenes. The poem in *The Revenge of the Pink Panther* was the great one in the Panthers. I got to,

'When duty calls,
You've got Balls!'

and Peter collapsed laughing. We kept going but eventually Blake had to get rid of him and he left the set! He really was a wonderful, wonderful giggler.

I was always rather proud of Peter. I used to think, good old Sellers - good old LAC. I have so many fond memories of him. I'd like him to be remembered with great affection and as a terrific film actor.

The man behind the mask has been 'surgically removed'.

Chapter 2

The Roar of the Greasepaint

'I could never be myself, there is no me . . . I do not exist!. . .
There used to be a me but I had it surgically removed'
Peter Sellers to Kermit, *The Muppet Show*, 1978

Legend has it that when Peter Sellers made his stage debut, the audience greeted him with thunderous applause and sang 'For He's A Jolly Good Fellow'. Sellers promptly started to cry. You could hardly blame him, though, because he was barely two weeks old at the time.

It was the middle of September 1925, and Richard Henry Sellers, as he would later be christened, had been carried on stage at the King's Theatre in Southsea by Dickie Henderson Snr. Peg and Bill Sellers watched from the wings as the birth of their son, who had arrived on 8 September, was announced to an appreciative crowd. They were both members of the variety company that was playing there, and Henderson was topping the bill.

Showbusiness was quite literally in the family blood and stretched back as far as the eighteenth century to Sellers' great great grandfather, the renowned and formidable pugilist, Daniel Mendoza. He was a boxer of tremendous skill and also a showman who enjoyed playing to his spectators, but in terms of true theatre, it was Mendoza's granddaughter who really began the family tradition.

Welcome Mendoza had a total of eight sons and two daughters who were all born after she was close to halfway through her fifth decade. When her husband, Solomon Marks, passed away she used a substantial amount of the money he left her to form a theatrical touring company by the name of Ray Brothers Limited, and all of her children became members of her troupe. She changed her own name to Ma Ray and set about creating a series of spectacular acts to attract the paying public to her shows. As Sellers later described, one performance came to a rather dramatic and totally unexpected end.

'There was this team of fiendish Germans who had invented a vast, portable water tank which could be secured to a stage, and you could watch people swimming around inside through its glass sides. Well, Ma Ray put on a revue that was called *Splash Me*, and it really was quite daring for its time, with a lot of scantily clad young chorus girls paddling around in formation in one of the tanks. During one of the matinees, the glass panel that faced the audience just shattered, because something had gone wrong with the water pressure.

'Suddenly, there was this massive tidal wave which flooded the orchestra pit and several of the girls landed on the laps of people sitting in the front few rows of the stalls, which also got drenched in the process. To this day, that story always conjures up an image in my mind of the trombonists in the band, with their mouthpieces pressed tightly to their lips, stretching the tips of their slides up above the water level so that they could breathe through them!'

Ma Ray's reputation for staging inventive and colourful shows quickly spread, and there was soon a huge demand for them from the provincial theatres. Such was her success that just prior to the outbreak of the First World War, she had dozens of touring companies working their way around the variety halls of England. As a result of all of this, she quickly acquired a nickname that stayed with her until the end of her days: The Queen of Spectacle.

No make-up, no disguises – a rare glimpse of Sellers off-duty.

One of the more daring routines that she devised was created as a vehicle for one of her daughters, Peg, and it was a performance that Sellers could vividly remember witnessing as a child. As he often recalled, it went something like this:

'The curtain would go up, and Mum would be standing there on a podium in front of a large white screen. All that she was wearing was a pale, almost flesh-coloured leotard, which gave the impression that she was completely starkers! Well, before any of the audience had managed to pick their jaws up off the floor from the shock of seeing this, my Uncle Bert, who was somewhere near the back of the stalls, turned on a glass plate projector which looked like some kind of ornate magic lantern, and a picture would envelop my mother.

'It created an illusion that made it look as though she'd become a character in a painting, and she would strike a pose that matched with the figure in the image. Suddenly, she was Florence Nightingale . . . Cleopatra . . . Queen Victoria. Anything was possible. I'd just stand there in the wings and listen to the gasps of sheer amazement and ripples of applause that greeted every change, as each slide merged into the next. It really was magical to watch.'

During the spring of 1921, Ma Ray's main company arrived in Portsmouth with a new water show called *Have A Dip!* By now, Peg was in her mid-twenties and still single - something that worried her mother to a certain degree, as she did not want to see one of her daughters being 'left on the shelf'. But that would soon change.

During an afternoon spent in one of the town's countless tea rooms, Ma Ray found herself hiring a new company member on the spot, after she'd seen how he managed to keep the clientele amused at a piano by playing a rendition of 'I'm Forever Blowing Bubbles' that sounded like a hymn. Bill Sellers had been the assistant organist at Bradford Cathedral, and when he agreed to double as both a driver and a pianist for Ma Ray, he quickly found himself on the Ray Brothers payroll.

One of his first assignments was to play the accompaniment during Peg's slideshow routine, and that was when the initial friendship that had grown between them started to become something more than just professional. The fact that Bill was a Protestant and Peg was Jewish didn't bother Ma in the slightest, and she happily gave the couple her blessing when he asked for her permission to marry her daughter some eighteen months later.

William and Agnes formally became husband and wife during a ceremony in the Bloomsbury Registry Office in 1923, but there was no time for a honeymoon. Peg was back on stage within a few hours, and Bill was playing his piano in the orchestra pit. Sellers once explained how that wasn't the only instrument that his father could play.

'Dad could pretty much get a tune out of anything from a banjo to a trumpet, and I never knew what the exact truth behind it was, but he used to boast about how he'd taught George Formby to play the ukulele . . .'

The young Peter Sellers was not impressed by the glamorous world of showbusiness. . .

To say that Sellers was his parents' only child is not strictly true, because Peg gave birth to another boy within a year of getting married. Tragically, he died when he was only a few months old. He was called Peter, and it was a name that passed on to her second son, even though he was registered as Richard. As with her first pregnancy, Peg insisted on carrying on with her stage work right up until the last possible moment. As Sellers once noted: 'Apparently, she only agreed not to go on when she felt the contractions starting, and even then, she was still waiting in the wings for her cue. Dad only just managed to get her back home in time . . .'

Bill and Peg were renting a tiny flat for the duration of the show's run, which sat on top of an equally diminutive shop by the name of Postcard Corner. It sold nothing but photographic and sketched views of the surrounding area's shipyards and docks, so it's hardly surprising that there was a very low turnover of stock.

Richard Henry was delivered by a local GP called Doctor Lytle, who was rather alarmed when Peg asked him if he thought it would be all right for her to go back to the theatre and appear in the following day's matinee performance. He told her that she should rest for at least three weeks. Peg only lasted out for one before she was back on the boards and touring with the show again.

When Dickie Henderson Snr held Sellers up to face his first audience, many of them must have thought how lucky the child was to have been born into the glamorous world of showbusiness. This was not the case at all, as Sellers' memories of his early years clearly illustrate:

'I hated the smell of sawdust that always hung around in the air backstage, or the stench of warm greasepaint and smoke that drifted off the performers as they spoke to me. You'd have a permanent sore throat from the fumes of the freshly painted scenery, oil lamps and gas bulbs, and there would be these awful stage managers who'd pat you on the head, pretending they knew who you were, even though they didn't have a clue, and near choking you with the smell of their beer-soaked whiskers and breath . . .'

Occasionally, Sellers would appear in the show, with his proper stage debut taking place when he was three years old. A top hat and tails suit in glistening white had been made for him, and with the orchestra subtly accompanying him, he'd swagger around singing 'My Old Dutch', a heavily sentimental song that had become the trademark tune of a comedian called Albert Chevalier. But although he may have enjoyed being on stage, he was far from happy with the fact that the only home life he knew was an unending succession of theatrical digs.

'The sheets always stank of starch and mothballs, and next to the rickety brass bed, with a mattress that always felt as though it had been stuffed with boulders, was a cracked marble washstand. It was always the same, no

. . .although later in life he enjoyed a glittering screen career. Here he repeats his role as Inspector Clouseau for the fifth time in *Revenge of the Pink Panther.*

matter where you went. In the front room of any boarding house, you could almost taste the heavy smell of floor wax and furniture polish that hung in the air, and the stench of boiling cabbage leaves drifting out of the kitchen is something that will always haunt me. I used to pray for the day to come when we'd have a home of our own . . .'

When Ma Ray died in 1932, her children decided to scale down the size of the company she'd been running. Over a period of about eighteen months or so, all bar one of their touring revues were closed down, and the best of the talent they had under contract was brought together to perform in what turned out to be the last of the Ray Brothers shows.

By 1935, a vast percentage of variety hall audiences were defecting en-masse to the growing number of cinemas that were opening across the country, and when they were faced with rapidly diminishing box-office returns as a consequence of this, the Rays were left with no alternative other than to dissolve the family business. Like several of her brothers, Peg decided to head for London with her own family and set about building up a new career as she came to terms with the fact that her days on stage were over.

While Peg rented a flat in Muswell Hill Road during the spring of the following year and took out a lease on a small antique-cum-junk shop nearby with her share of the assets from the Ray Brothers coffers, Bill Sellers opted to set off on tour again. He joined forces with a friend called Arthur Lewis and formed a ukulele act, which they took around the coastal resorts of the country performing in whatever venues they could find. Peter, meanwhile, was starting his rather erratic schooling at this point. Initially, he attended St Mark's Kindergarten on the outskirts of Camden Town, but because of his

An erratic schooling and unsettled start did nothing to stunt Sellers' genius for comedy, encapsulated in his portrayal of Inspector Clouseau.

Tea break on *The Mouse That Roared*, a hilarious vehicle for Sellers' talents.

mother's habit of frequently moving house, he never had a settled educational base. The last of nearly a dozen establishments he attended was the St Alyosius College in Hornsey Lane, which was run by the Brothers of Our Lady of Mercy. In a bizarre move, which Sellers would later often joke about, the son of Protestant/Jewish parents was receiving Catholic tutelage. Sellers certainly remembered the monks as being sportsmen of extreme cunning.

'Football games in the playground would often turn into tactical exercises as we tried to figure out how to outmanoeuvre the Brothers. They'd hoist up their cassocks and tuck them into these thick brown belts that they wore, and that gave them the freedom to run around our makeshift pitch with all the grace and skill of a seasoned professional. If we ever managed to score, they'd get their own back by dropping their skirts down over the ball, and there'd be no way for us to get it back off them until they'd equalised . . .'

At weekends, Sellers would accompany his mother and whichever uncle she'd managed to procure transportation from, and head for the outer suburbs of

London. The fact of the matter was that Peg needed antiques and trinkets to sell in her shop, and she had to acquire them as cheaply as possible because money was tight. So she'd pose as a director from the London Gold Refining Company and call from door to door, offering bogus valuations on any pieces of gold and silver that the householders might have.

After conjuring up what she thought to be a reasonable price, Peg would then offer to buy the items from them and if they agreed, they'd be polished and on display in her shop window within a few days. Suffice to say that the difference between what she purchased them for and what she was selling them for was quite considerable, and in her favour. Sellers always marvelled at the techniques his mother employed.

'She had her patter down to a fine art, and nothing ever seemed to throw her. Even when people started to get suspicious and began asking awkward questions, she always managed to maintain an aloof air of detachment and keep the pretence going. Sometimes, it paid off handsomely and she'd get a piece that would help to pay the rent for a week once she'd sold it, but equally, there could be days when the only thing that she'd be shown was a door slamming in her face . . .'

After the outbreak of the Second World War in September 1939, it was announced that St Aloysius would be closing. As a result, many of the school's

Sellers maintains his own 'aloof air of detachment'.

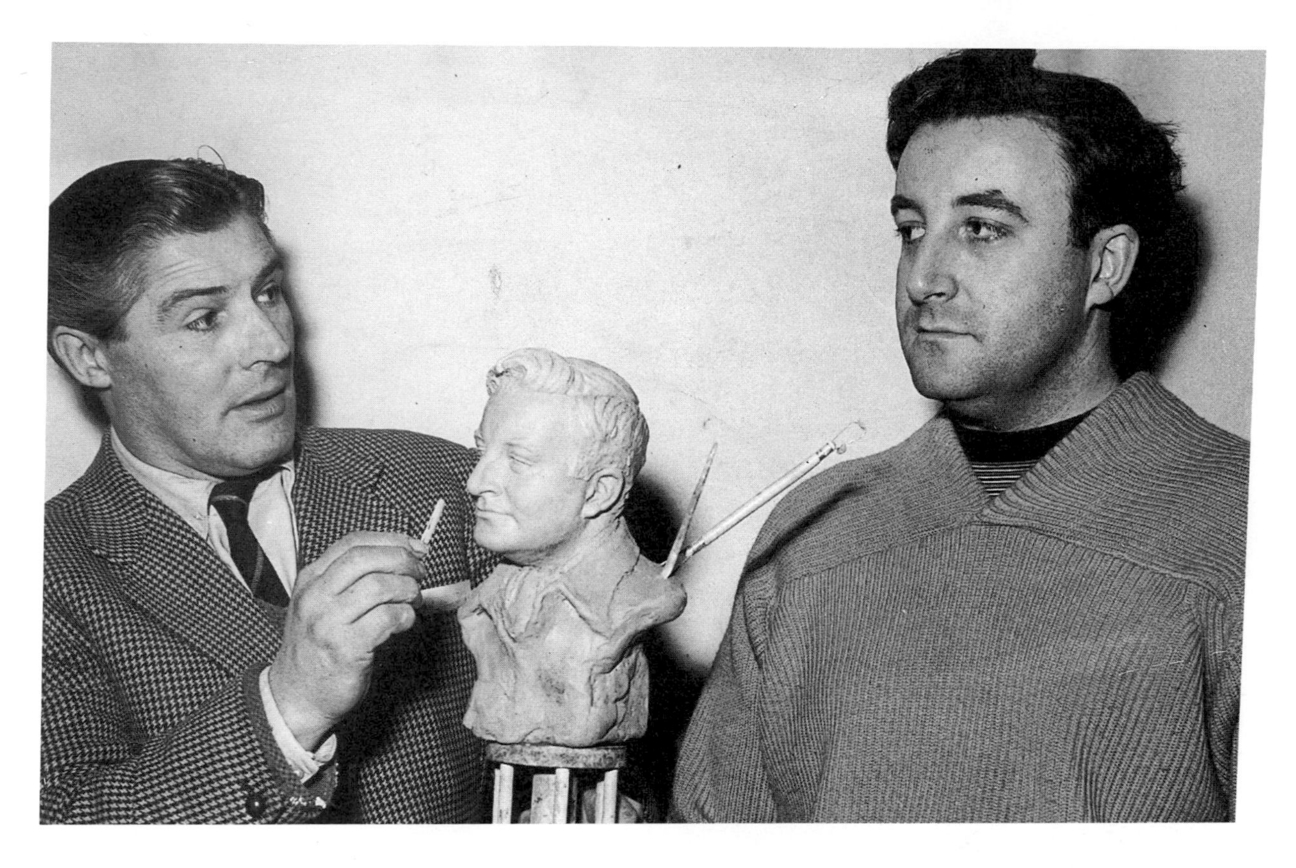

pupils became evacuees. When a stray German bomb levelled Peg's shop, she decided it was time for her to bring her family back together and head for the safety of the coast. Bill, who'd been away for over a year, gave up touring and joined his wife and son as they made the move from London to Ilfracombe, where family connections had secured them work at the Victoria Pavilion Theatre.

Sellers was just thirteen years old, and his departure from the capital also brought an end to his education. The reason for this was quite simple - he found the mystique of working in the theatre that he had so detested as a child completely enthralling, and was soon so immersed in the plethora of backstage

Peg Sellers could have asked a huge price for her own son's likeness in clay.

jobs that he didn't bother going back to school. Later on in life, he often admitted that he deeply regretted this fact and that as a result, he only ever felt half educated.

While his mother sold tickets at the box office and his father worked in the orchestra pit, Sellers did everything from cleaning the stage and sticking up bill posters to painting the sets and arranging the lighting. Within a few months, he'd been promoted to the rank of assistant stage manager and began treading the boards as an actor for the first time, with tiny supporting roles consisting of no

Peter Sellers

Sellers pursued an early career as a drummer.

more than a few lines of dialogue.

The Victoria Pavilion's programme of entertainment changed two or three times a month as touring plays and bands came and went, with the stalls easily being cleared to make way for a dancefloor when such things were required. Sellers would watch the visiting musical groups from the wings, paying particular attention to the drummers:

'The technicalities of playing the drums always fascinated me, and one week a brilliant act by the name of *Joe Daniels And His Hotshots* took to the stage. They had a vast drum kit, and I just couldn't resist it . . . I had to have a go. So every night I sat there until the early hours, bashing out any rhythm that came into my head to an empty auditorium, but then I got caught. Rather than complain to the management and try to get me sacked, Joe Daniels actually told me to shift over and he sat down and started to show me what I was doing wrong. He gave me lessons, and by the end of the week I was good enough for him to let me sit in with the band, and play along with them as best I could . . .'

Professional tuition soon followed with the gift of his own £200 kit from his parents, and before long Sellers was able to supplement his own income from the theatre by playing with several dance bands during his evenings off. One was led by the great Waldini, who was actually a flamboyant Welshman called Wally Bishop, and he insisted that all of his musicians dress as nomadic troubadours.

Work with Henry Hall and Oscar Rabin's orchestras would soon follow, but before any of that happened Sellers hit the road with his father, as Bill went back on tour again during the summer of 1942. An acrobat, a singer and a dancer all crammed themselves into a tiny rusting van with a piano strapped to its back, as both Sellers Senior and Junior took turns in driving their makeshift revue around the country, all in the name of ENSA.

They were now part of a vast network of variety companies that put on shows to entertain munitions workers and soldiers, who affectionately dubbed their abbreviated title as standing for Every Night Something Awful. Sellers would play his drums or ukulele, which his father was teaching him to play, and then finish off his act with a few impressions of the famous radio stars of the day, such as Tommy Handley and Jack Train from ITMA.

One particular venue they played at was in Taunton, and due to a double booking at a guest house, it looked as though they'd have to spend the night sleeping in Bill's van. Salvation came in the form of ENSA's local area manager, who offered them free accommodation in his own home. What he failed to mention was the fact that he was also the local undertaker and that several of his clients would also be stopping over. Sellers takes up the story, and explains how it led to his first intimate contact with a member of the opposite sex.

'We called the place Castle Frankenstein, because he did all of the embalming in his cellar and had three occupied coffins in the front room. I've got to admit that it wasn't only the girls that were touring with us who thought the place was as creepy as hell. So, when one of them confessed that she was too scared to sleep on her own and hinted that her door would be left unlocked, just in case I felt like comforting her during the night . . . Well, what else was a young man to do? She was a few years older

Bill Sellers taught his son to play the ukulele.

While serving in the RAF, Sellers (fourth from right) brought his chameleon-like qualities to the *Gang Show*. . .

than me, and could probably hear my hormones squeaking, but that didn't matter at all as far as I was concerned.

'Armed with the best Robert Donat impression that I could muster, which had been proved to melt a girl's heart from fifty paces during previous field tests, I crept into her bedroom at about two o'clock in the morning, complete with pyjamas, dressing gown and a fine silk cravat. The mistake I made was in not taking them off before I got into bed with her. When you've got that much on, and there's also numerous sheets to contend with, it's a bit like trying to make love in a straightjacket . . . So the whole thing was a bit of a disaster, especially when I fell on the floor and badly bruised my back. It wasn't only the corpses in the house who were stiff for the rest of that night!'

Twenty years later, Sellers told Blake Edwards the same story while they were shooting *The Pink Panther* on location in Rome. The director quickly worked a similar scenario into the script, and Sellers found himself having to relive the same tangled situation as he acted out Clouseau's abortive amorous advances towards his wife, who was being played by Capucine.

Not long after the Taunton incident, Sellers decided to leave the ENSA tour and went to join his mother, who was now living in Brighton. To help pay for her lodgings, Peg had restarted the London Gold Refining Company operation and when Sellers arrived, he helped to support his family by working as a drummer in the local dance halls. This was during the spring of 1943 and by

. . .and after the war honed them to perfection in *The Goon Show*.

September, when Sellers celebrated his eighteenth birthday, the inevitable happened.

Airman Second Class, No. 2223033, Sellers, P. began his active service with the RAF after being conscripted, and started out with the lowly job of working on aircraft-hand ground duties, which basically meant that he had to load bullets into fighter planes. His poor eyesight prevented him from being able to train as a pilot, so it looked as though he'd be spending the duration counting out ammunition, but then an opportunity presented itself that offered him an escape route from such monotony.

Prior to the war, the unrelenting ebullient Ralph Reader had been the driving force behind the boy scouts' acclaimed variety revues, which were known as *Gang Shows*. Reader was now a squadron leader in the RAF, and applied his producing skills to staging

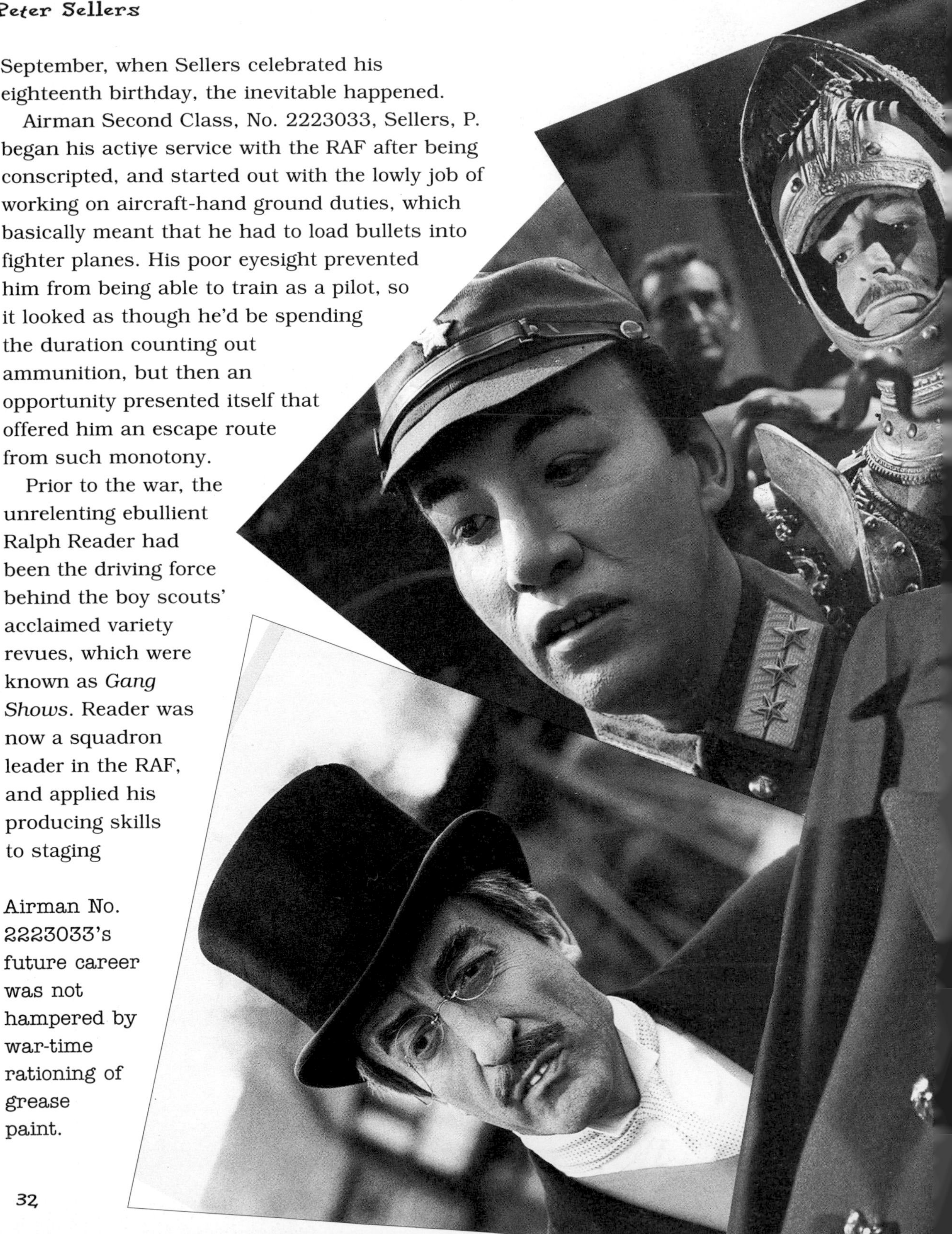

Airman No. 2223033's future career was not hampered by war-time rationing of grease paint.

Sellers as the second-rate Matador explaining the main points of bull-fighting in *The Bobo*.

concerts which toured around the Royal Air Force encampments throughout the world. Because of the Reader connection, they were also known as *Gang Shows*, and a certain young airman heard that they were always on the lookout for volunteers.

Sellers had a successful audition and quickly found himself being transferred to *Gang Show No. 10*, which took him on postings to Ceylon, Burma and India over the course of the next two years. As soon as he was abroad, Sellers started conducting some potentially dangerous experiments as he began to explore how far he could go with his natural ability to do uncanny vocal and sometimes physical impersonations.

His new unit's costume hampers were a treasure trove of different military uniforms, and even though supplies of greasepaint were sparse, Sellers still had access to all that he needed to be able to bring his plan to life. A new breed of chameleon had been unleashed within the ranks of the *Gang Show*, and only a select few friends knew exactly what he was up to - and it terrified them.

Whenever their concert party arrived at a new transit camp, peculiar reports began to circulate detailing the unannounced arrival of a high-ranking official at some point during their stay. Word had it that he'd either put in an appearance at the officers' mess, or simply walk into one of the barrack rooms for an informal chat with some of the troops.

Rumours suggested that these people varied from being a Sikh flying officer to an elderly British general, and because they spanned such nationalities, no one ever thought they could possibly be the same man. Even if they did hazard a guess along those lines, the thought of the kind of jail sentences that resulted from masquerading as such high ranks probably made them want to forget about the idea immediately. Twenty-five years later, Airman No. 2223033 confessed to what had been going on:

'I wanted to find out what it would be like to spend an evening in the mess, instead of the canteen, and seeing as there was little hope of me ever being promoted to an officer, the only way for me to get in there was in disguise. So that's what I did, and after a while I realised that I could immerse myself in a character so completely that people couldn't recognise who I really was.

'It worked so well because there was never an accurate record of who should or shouldn't have been in the grounds of the camps that we played at, so no questions were ever asked about any extra personnel, especially when they were as senior as the ones that I camouflaged myself as. There was also a safety margin

In *The Pink Panther* Sellers drew from his own experiences as he acted out Clouseau's abortive amorous advances towards his wife, played by Capucine

involved, because no subordinate rank would have ever accused an officer of being an imposter, let alone a general, even if it was blatantly obvious. I made sure that I was only ever seen as figures of respect, such as a wing commander or a group captain, and it all became rather addictive after a while. I was always setting myself challenges to try and top my last performance . . .'

There seemed to be no limit to his inventiveness with his make-up kit, and even after he'd managed to pull off an impersonation of an Indian officer, complete with a turban and beard, it still seemed as though he wouldn't be satisfied until his characterisations had taken him to the very top of the RAF's hierarchy. The closest he ever came to getting caught was on Christmas Eve 1944.

'The most audacious thing that I ever did was probably the riskiest as well, because I pretended to be an air commodore and walked straight into a blisteringly drunk air marshal in the bar room at the mess, and he became convinced that I knew an old friend of his called 'Tedders'. He kept peering into my face, and I was certain that sooner or later he'd see that I was about forty years too young to have reached that kind of rank, so I began to panic.

'The perspiration that was pouring off my forehead was starting to turn the talcum powder that I'd greyed my temples with into dough, so I suggested that we gave 'Tedders' a festive toast in order to create a diversion. By the time the air marshal had turned back to face me from the bar, armed with two loaded glasses, I was already in the sergeants' mess next door, giving them a rousing speech to hide my nerves that Churchill himself would have been proud of . . .'

Sellers' brain must have gone into overdrive during his time in the Air Force, because he loved to observe people and try to absorb and memorise all of the different accents and character traits that he encountered on his travels. Every gesture or mannerism that struck him as being unusual or interesting was filed away in his memory, safely stored as future reference points for him to work from. His knack of being able to perfectly reproduce every vocal inflection of a person that he'd only met a few minutes before later earned him a reputation among friends as 'The Man With A Tape Recorder In His Head', which was actually a very accurate metaphor for him.

When the war came to an end the following summer, Sellers returned to England to collect his demob suit and ration book, and moved in with his parents, who were now living in a flat in Finchley. Its close proximity to the capital made life easier for their son - who had decided to restart his civilian life by going back into showbusiness with the act that he'd developed in the *Gang Show* - because much of his time was spent going to see the London-based variety agents in an attempt to win bookings for a routine that he simply described as 'Drums and Impressions'. It proved to be far from easy.

A week's engagement at the Empire Theatre in Peterborough turned into a

Sellers could never resist the call of the drums.

nightmare during the opening night, when Sellers was booed off the stage by the audience midway through his act. It was only thanks to the intervention of the show's star, singer Dorothy Squires, that saved him from being sacked on the spot by the venue's manager. It was an experience that haunted Sellers for the rest of his life.

'There's no way to really describe the feeling of sheer terror that you get when you're hit by a wave of hatred like that. It left me shaking, and by the time that I'd made it back to my dressing room I felt physically sick. That night hammered home the fact that there's a big difference between being able to keep the general public amused and making a few soldiers laugh. I think it's safe to say that the whole thing was a bit of a confidence shatterer . . .'

After leaving a band called The Jive Bombers, Sellers decided to make drumming more of a sideline career and concentrate on trying to find a wider audience for his own particular brand of comedy. But the question was how. It wouldn't be that long before he managed to find the answer . . .

Dennis Selinger

Dennis Selinger was Sellers' agent and friend for forty years

I was Peter's agent for more or less 40 years. I first met him in India. I was in the RAF and he came out with the *Gang Show*.

Then when I came out of the service in 1945 I got a call from Peggy, his mother, asking if I would go down to Jersey to see her son Peter, who was then Entertainments Manager at a holiday camp, and I went down and saw him. I didn't realise at the time that I'd met him out in India. He was doing a stand-up comedy act and MC-ing the show. He finished up with an impression of George Formby, otherwise he was telling stories in dialects. I thought he was very funny and that's when I started to represent him.

He really was amazing with voices. Twentieth Century Fox made a picture called *The Black Rose* (1950) starring Tyrone Power. They phoned me out of the blue and asked if Peter would do some revoicing on it, because there was a Chinese bandit played by an actor who had a strong Mexican accent which sounded very strange. Peter was keen as he wasn't in films in those days, and we did a deal. They sent him a tape of the film and he did an excellent job. Some time later I got a call from Twentieth Century Fox asking if Mr Sellers was still available because they wanted him to redo the voice. I asked what the problem was and they said it was so like the original they needed him to do it again! He got paid again to redo it.

He always said that he fashioned Bloodnok on me! That's why he called him DENNIS Bloodnok. He used to say things like that and with Peter you never quite knew if they were true - not that it mattered. He also said that Fred Kite in *I'm All Right, Jack* was very much fashioned on me, with the little moustache and sleek hair just like I had in those days.

Whenever he was depressed he would go right back to *The Goon Show*, in that he would phone up Spike, Harry, Mike Bentine, Graham Stark or myself. I think it was probably his way of recapturing one of the happiest periods of his life. He was terribly nostalgic about The Goons.

I remember he phoned me up one Saturday evening and asked me to go out for supper. I picked him up in my new car, a Ford Cortina with a Lotus engine and I'd had the top chopped off - it was the only one like it. We had a lovely supper and suddenly he said, 'Get the bill, we're going. Can I drive the car back?' He had raved about the car on the way there. He was an Advanced Motorist and a good driver. I've been round Le Mans track with Steve McQueen and it didn't scare me but this did! Peter drove like a maniac through the West End of London, screamed up, got out, slammed the door and disappeared. The next day Theo Cowan brought me a letter from Peter, I still have it, it said to the effect,

My dear Den, It was great having supper with you last night and I've come to the conclusion that clearly you are dotty with power and I would rather remain your friend forever more than ever have to do business with you again. Yours as ever, Pete.

I was amazed but I decided not to do anything. I phoned Theo the next day to tell him about the letter. I said that I refused to ring Peter, and I would carry on as per normal as we had a contract. I asked him to query what Peter meant by 'clearly dotty with power.'

He relayed the message back to Peter who said, 'We had a lovely supper and were talking about the business, and he kept talking about Sam Spiegel, Harry Saltzman and Cubby Broccoli, but he never mentioned the Boulting Brothers.' That was that, it was all forgotten five minutes later. He was absolutely fed up because I had mentioned all these high-powered producers, but not the Boulting Brothers.

When he was doing the play Brouhaha in 1958 I used to get phone calls from the management every five seconds saying, 'he's done it again!' It was a nightmare. He hated doing stage. He just wanted to do something different for every performance. He went out front each night to say a bit about the character and the play, and one night he went out and said in the Sheikh's voice, 'Ladies and Gentlemen, I've just come from Buckingham Palace where a dear friend of mine received his knighthood today, Sir Alec Guinness, and we had a couple of glasses of champagne to celebrate and I have to tell you now that I'm drunk out of my mind so if you want to go and get your money back, I suggest you do it now!'

Another time he fell off the stage and went straight into the drum! He was doing the Tango and got carried away. And then there was the night he went on and took pictures of the cast performing with his new 8mm camera. Luckily, the cast were marvellous. I had these wonderful phone conversations with the management, who were sticklers for discipline. He had a six month contract and the theatre was packed from the time they opened - it did tremendous business.

A lot of Peter's performances are memorable but I know he would want to be remembered for *Being There*. He always wanted to be known as a dramatic actor and he proved himself in that film. He was wonderful, as good as anyone could ever be. He was terribly upset that he didn't get the Oscar for it. I believe quite honestly that was one of the reasons why he finally gave up; he was so disappointed.

He was extraordinarily generous in a lot of ways. When I think of Peter I think of the friendship I had with him, which did have its ups and downs - but many more ups than downs. I miss him. We had so many laughs. We had a great time together.

Tony Hancock – another great British comedian who, like Sellers, did a stint at the Windmill Theatre.

Chapter 3

Beautiful Mind Plays

'What is a goon? A goon is someone with a one-cell brain . . . Anything that is not basically simple puzzles a goon . . . his language is inarticulate. . . He thinks in the fourth dimension . . .'
James Thomas, radio critic, *The News Cronicle*, 1951

'We'd like to offer a reminder to all of our patrons that the use of binoculars, or any other kind of artificial aid to vision, is strictly prohibited whilst any of the ladies of the chorus are present on stage and in a state of undress . . .'

This, according to Sellers, was the kind of announcement that could frequently be heard echoing through the auditorium of the Windmill Theatre, which was to be found buried deep in the heart of Piccadilly Circus in central London. Like so many other comedians from his generation, including Tony Hancock and future fellow goons Harry Secombe and Michael Bentine, he spent a gruelling six-week season there trying to raise a laugh from the mainly sweaty, dirty raincoated clientele who inhabited the stalls.

Peter Sellers' name was listed as being part of the bill performing in the 211th edition of *Revudeville*, which was one of the legendary shows staged at the Windmill by Vivian Van Damm, a producer whose creative skills knew no bounds when it came to flagrantly flaunting the loophole that had been discovered in the rather draconian censorship laws of the time.

Michael Bentine thinking in the fourth dimension.

The rules, as instigated and supervised by Lord Chamberlain's office, stipulated that human nudity was only acceptable for public exhibition when the subject involved was something like a classic work of art. This meant that famous paintings or statues could be put on display in museums, etc., without fear of prosecution, and it also gave Van Damm the idea to create an establishment that would become as infamous as it was popular, as Sellers later explained.

'Van Damm figured out that he could use nude models to pose in mock-ups of famous pictures on stage, and that the legal system couldn't touch him as long as he ensured that they kept perfectly still. As far as he was concerned, it was living art and representative of something that was already on view to the public . . . It was a bulletproof scam!

'So, he hired ladies of ample proportions in just the right places, although some of them needed body stockings and the odd strategically placed strip of gaffer tape to help them achieve such an effect, and had them drape themselves around a set in an attempt to recreate great moments from history or art. For instance, Julius Caesar could be seen addressing a predominantly female and togaless senate, whilst completely failing to notice the fact that he'd acquired a pair of female breasts, even though he was wearing little more than a laurel wreath himself . . . You get the idea?

'While all of the scene changes were taking place behind the stage curtains, it was up to one of the comedians to take it in turns and wade across the saliva-strewn floor, courtesy of the front three rows and their wishful thinking, and try to keep the audience amused until the Mona Lisa came on, revealing far more than just her enigmatic smile. Can you imagine what it was like trying to follow on and top something like that?

'One moment the audience was staring

An early mugshot: Peter Sellers – drummer and impressionist.

boggle-eyed at six provocatively sprawled young ladies, re-enacting 'The Charge of the Light Brigade' with a handful of feather boas, and before they knew it, they were suddenly being verbally assaulted by a Brylcreemed bag of nerves in an ill-fitting suit who was cracking the most appalling jokes. It went on like that for six shows a day, in an atmosphere of cigarette smoke and pheromones that you could cut with a knife. Any laughs that we got were probably due to suppressed tension!'

The Windmill Theatre was seen by many as a training ground for comedians, where they could develop and hone their routines. Sellers concentrated on impersonations, which varied from a pastiche of Sidney Greenstreet and Peter Lorre in *The Maltese Falcon*, which he was still quite happy to reprise on chat shows up until his death, to a bizarre sketch where he walked on stage wearing long johns, a tutu, a Viking helmet with a huge beard bristling under his chin, a boxing glove and army boots, while carrying a stuffed crocodile under his free arm. This, he would calmly announce, was planned to be his definitive impression of the young Queen Victoria on holiday in Bognor Regis, but there was a problem . . . he'd forgotten what she looked like!

If nothing else came from working at the venue, then there was practically a guarantee that the activities of certain patrons would at least give you a good anecdote to tell for years to come. One story that Sellers was fond of telling involved the lengths that one man went to in trying to outwit the 'No Binoculars' house rule.

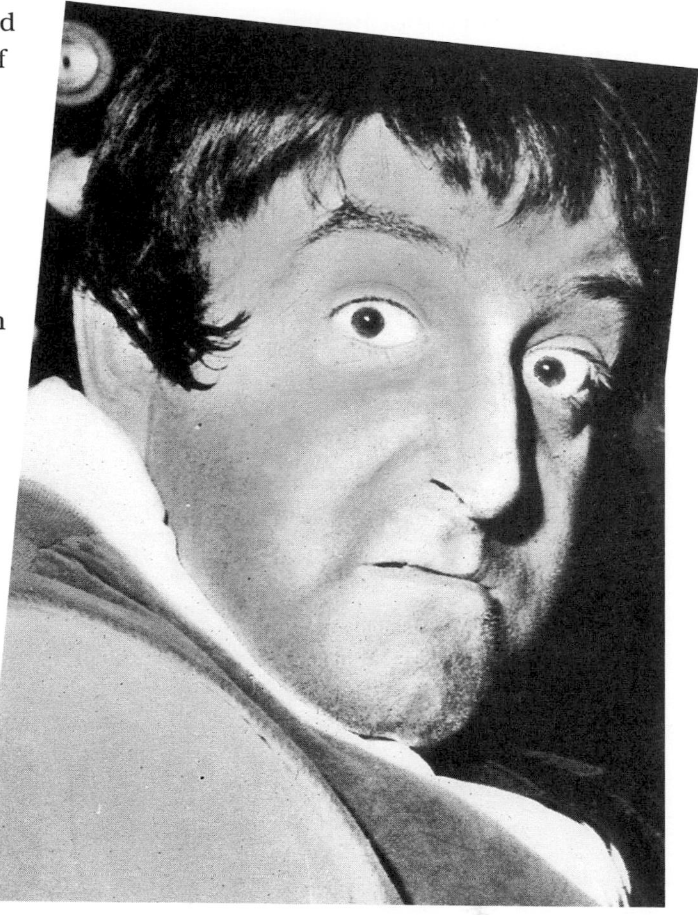

An intermediate mugshot – Peter Sellers – tom thumb.

'There was one inventive old pervert who spent an absolute fortune on having a pair of glasses made with lenses like telescopes. They looked like the bottoms of milk bottles and had such extreme magnification that you could probably look up a gnat's nostrils from a hundred yards away. Well, this guy managed to get past the doorman, and even the ushers failed to notice that he was wearing them, but as soon as he tried to walk down the steps leading to the stalls, his exaggerated depth of vision got the better of him.

'He tripped, yelped and flew through the air at an alarming speed before breaking both his fall and his legs on the front of the stage. The thing was that as the ambulancemen were carrying him away on a stretcher, he called the doorman over and quietly asked him for his money back because he hadn't seen any of the show . . .'

Sellers was earning £25 a week for his efforts, so in purely financial terms the run that he was booked for at the Windmill from March through to April 1948 was certainly one of the most lucrative periods that he'd experienced since being demobbed, because there had been some fairly lean times up to that point. His main source of income had been through going back to working as a drummer for hire, or spending extended summer seasons in the more distant English holiday resorts, such as Jersey.

To make ends meet towards the end of his first year back in civilian life, he'd even taken on a job as a fairground barker, and used the best W.C. Fields take-off he could muster to try and lure the public in to see the fat bearded ladies and the Siamese twins. This did little to mentally challenge or stimulate Sellers' vivid imagination, so he resorted to his old Air Force tricks to relieve the boredom by pretending to be a figure of respect. Only this time he got caught . . .

It all began when he travelled to

Airman 2223033 re-incarnated behind enemy lines.

Norwich to visit his then current girlfriend, Hilda Parkin, and registered at the most elite hotel in the area under the alias of Lord Beaconsfield. Suffice to say, the staff were the epitome of subservience and practically rolled out the red carpet to greet him, but their mood soon changed, as Sellers later revealed.

'When I got there, they were offering me free champagne breakfasts, hot and cold running chambermaids, the works . . . But as soon as I checked in after spending an afternoon in the town, the manager asked me if I'd mind stepping into his office for a quiet word and before I knew it, I was pinned down on his desk top by two pinstriped MOD gorillas who thought they'd caught a deserter.

'It turned out that the maids had found a handful of old Woodbines and a shirt from Woolworth's when they unpacked my case, and in the manager's eyes, that did not equate with an entry in Burke's Peerage, so he did some checking, came to the conclusion that I was an imposter of the highest order and called in for the heavy mob. To avoid any further confusion, I used words of no more than two syllables to explain that I was ex-RAF and merely playing a joke. The gorillas soon lost interest when they realised there'd be no more violence and let me go, but that was certainly the last time that I ever tried pulling that stunt!'

Sellers was beginning to feel that his career was going nowhere fast, so he decided to try and break into the relatively new medium of television. After writing to the booking manager at the BBC's HQ, the famed Alexandra Palace in north London, he soon found himself being auditioned in 'TV studio conditions' and as a result of this, he made his debut on the small screen in a variety show called *New To You* on 18 March 1948, the day after he'd opened at the Windmill.

Sellers' artistry as a mimic got him his first break in radio: he used his Kenneth Horne (above) impersonation to recommend his own talents to a senior radio producer over the phone.

His roll call of movie star impersonations went down well enough to warrant a return appearance on the same programme during the following week, but it hardly brought him overnight stardom. The actual number of people who owned television sets at that time was minute compared to the sheer volume who possessed radios, so getting his voice on the airwaves seemed to be the next obvious step to take.

An audition before the austere BBC Radio board of adjudicators was quickly arranged to take place on 1 April that year, and even though the panel he faced deemed him ideally suited for inclusion in their variety output, nothing seemed to happen. Frustration set in as the weeks of silence on the BBC's part turned into months, and with no apparent signs of any potential employment emerging from the corporation, Sellers decided to do something that was tantamount to committing career suicide.

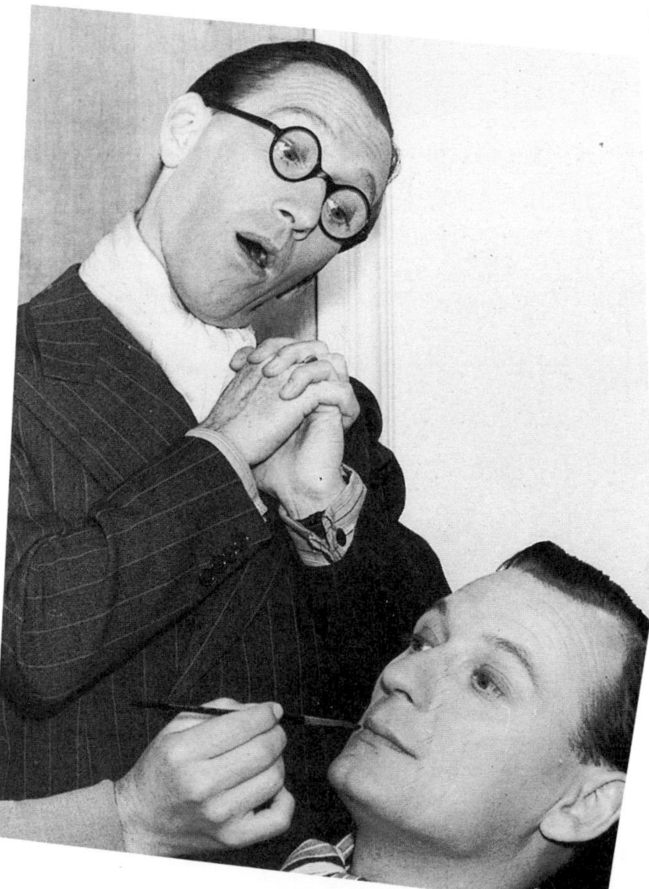

Arthur Askey and Dickie Murdoch in the studio while filming *Band Waggon.*

'I phoned the BBC because I was determined to plead my case to Roy Speer, who was one of their senior radio producers, even though I knew I had a snowball's chance in hell of getting through to him as myself. So I brought my best Kenneth Horne impersonation into play, with a neat imitation of Dickie Murdoch as back up . . .'

Although he's now best remembered for *Beyond Our Ken* and *Round the Horne* during the 1960s, Horne was in partnership with Murdoch at the time, who had a long association with Arthur Askey as his straight man, and they were starring in and writing the bulk of *Much Binding In The Marsh*, which was a staple part of the public's radio listening diet for over a decade.

'And when I got through to the switchboard I said, "Kenneth Horne here, put me through to Roy Speer," and to my utter amazement his secretary was on the line in the next instant, so I kept going. "Kenneth Horne speaking. I wonder if I could have a word with Roy?" Perspiration began to run off me like a waterfall when he came on the line and said, "Hello, Ken. What can we do for you?" It's probably safe to say that if I'd put my career up the creek without a paddle by that point, then the boat began to sink over the course of the next few moments . . .

'I told him that Dickie Murdoch was there as well and said, "We thought we ought to let you know that we saw a young fellow on stage the other night. Now, what was his name, Dickie?" "Sellers," I said, answering myself. "The name was Peter Sellers." "Oh, yes!" enthused Horne, "A marvellous impersonator. You ought to get him on one of your shows . . ."

'I could swear that I heard Speer actually writing my name down, and that's when my nerve finally evaporated and I said, "It's me." There was a deafening silence on the other line. "It's me . . . I'm Peter Sellers. I was wondering whether I could have a spot on your programme." That's when flames started to curl around the receiver. "What! You cheeky young bugger! Well, you certainly had me fooled! You'd better come round and we'll see if we can fix something up." And with that, he hung up. I'm pretty certain that if I hadn't made that call, I'd still be waiting to hear from the BBC to this day.'

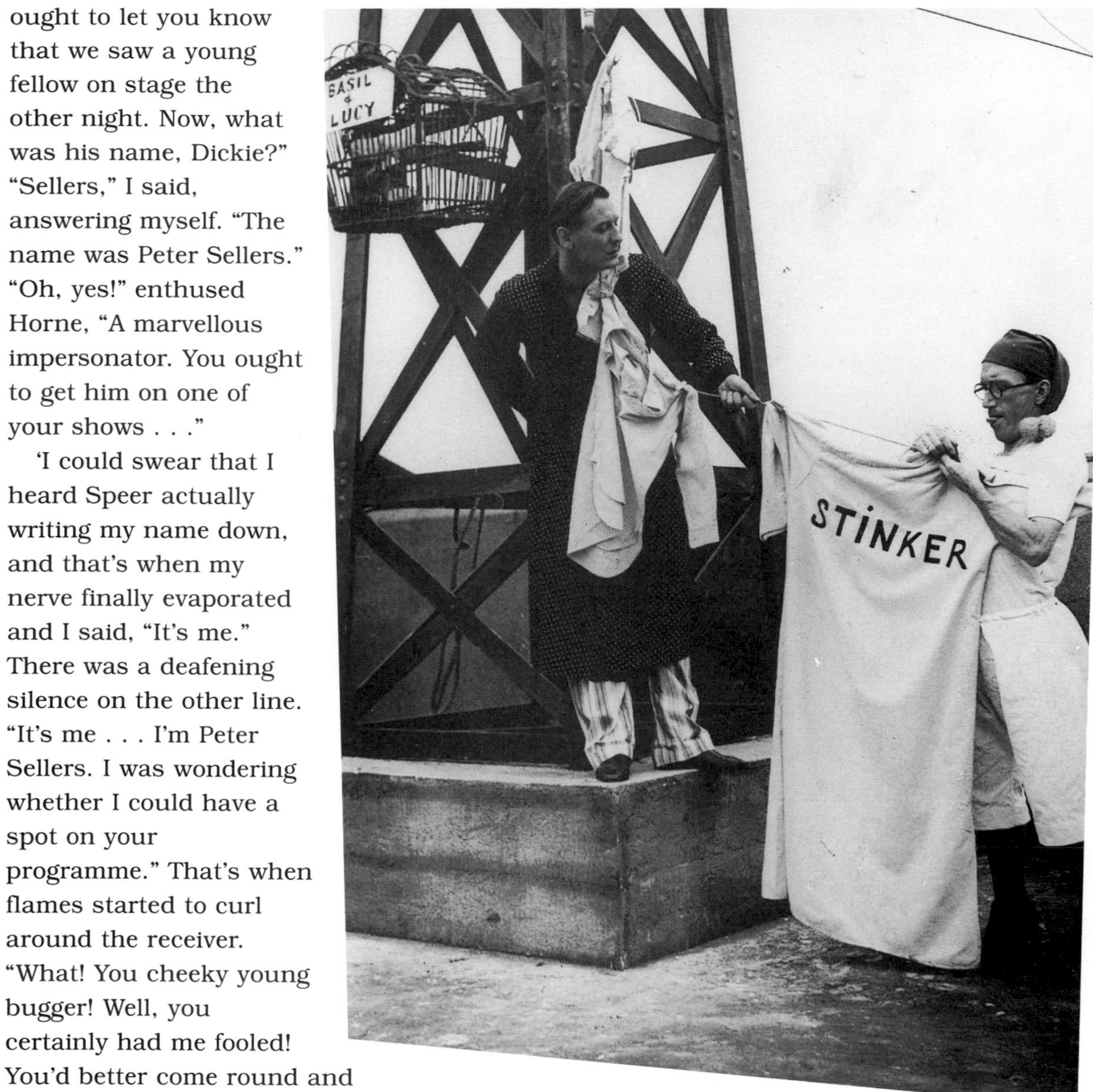

'Stinker' Murdoch and Big-Hearted Arthur on the set of *Band Waggon.*

Sellers' gamble paid off because Speer promptly booked him to appear in a Dick Bentley-hosted series called *Show Time*, and the 210 seconds he spent performing a sketch, co-written with his father, detailing the chaotic efforts of a foreigner as he tries to learn English from a shortwave radio set, changed the course

Dickie Murdoch departing from the BBC to make a commercial

of his career for ever. The show was broadcast during the evening of 1 July 1948 and ecstatic reviews praising his work began to appear in the press about a week or so after transmission.

As a result of this, a newspaper headline reading 'This Comic Is Tops!' was one of the first cuttings that Peg Sellers was able to glue into a recently purchased green leather-bound scrapbook, and the pages quickly began to fill up as offers of work flooded in for her son. Every major variety show on the airwaves seemed to be fighting to secure the services of Peter Sellers as a guest star. Another stint on *Show Time* came on 19 August, with a similar spot on *It's Fine To Be Young* at the end of the month, along with the first of eleven consecutive weekly appearances on *Starlight Hour.*

By the end of October, apart from being heard on programmes such as Henry Hall's *Guest Night* and the radio incarnation of *The Gang Show*, Sellers also became a regular on *Tempo For Today* and *Variety Bandbox.*

Suddenly, the money was rolling in and he found that he was now able to start indulging a passion that had been financially out of his reach up until that point.

'If it's got four wheels, an engine and a gear stick, then there's a fair chance that I've owned or at the very least driven one at some point during my life. Gadgets and mechanical gizmos of all shapes and sizes have always been my Achilles' heel . . . especially cars. Before I'd managed to make a breakthrough on the radio, it was a case of trying to find an honest-looking dealer down one of the north London side streets, and then praying that you'd make it home before the engine blew up on whatever the make of rust-bucket was that he'd conned you into buying.

'So, after experiencing that kind of thing on more than one occasion it felt slightly surreal when I was suddenly able to go into one of the showrooms around Hyde Park and not only sit in the vehicle beforehand, but also take it out for a test drive. To me, that was really the first sign that success had finally arrived.'

The image of the seedy camel-coated dealers, with their pencil-line moustaches and battered brown trilbys, was something that always stayed in Sellers' memory. During the latter stages of his film career, one pet project that remained unrealised would have involved him bringing his own rendition of a downmarket car salesman to life on screen, with the character being named after one of the main roads in London where Sellers had encountered the real thing decades before: Warren Street.

The BBC, meanwhile, had begun to realise that their new star's considerable potential was not being fully realised by restricting his appearances to just variety shows. It became quite clear that his characterisation skills could be put to even greater use elsewhere, so Sellers was drafted in as a cast member of a

Sellers in commercial mode as Thrifty McTravel – one of the many characters he created to help advertise TWA.

new sketch-driven radio series called *Third Division*. The scripts were fresh from the pens of Frank Muir and Dennis Norden and the shows were due to be recorded in the run up to Christmas that year.

Although it's now little more than a dim and distant memory, even for those who were directly involved, there are two main reasons why *Third Division* was important as far as Sellers is concerned. First, the second episode of the show's six-week run saw him performing alongside Benny Hill and Patricia Hayes in a sketch called 'Balham - Gateway To The South', which Sellers would later record for commercial release and with great success as a solo routine some ten years later during 1958.

Second, during an early script meeting, the show's producer, Pat Dixon, made a point of introducing Sellers to two of his fellow performers, thinking that they

Frank Muir and Denis Norden go through one of their scripts with Dick Bentley.

Comedian Benny Hill, who performed alongside Sellers in *Third Division*, at home assessing the competition.

might get on together as they were also former 'Windmill Boys'. No one could have predicted what this would lead to . . .

Shortly after being demobbed in 1946, Harry Secombe's quest to gain experience in the entertainment industry led him along the same path that Sellers later followed when he arrived at Vivian Van Damm's doorstep for an audition. He also won a six-week contract in one of the Revudeville shows, and as that particular tour of theatrical duty was coming to an end, Secombe spent an afternoon in the stalls of the Windmill watching the dress rehearsal for the next *Revudeville*, which was due to open as soon as his show closed during the course of the following week.

The crazy antics of one particular double act appealed to Secombe's sense of the absurd, and when the run-through was over he went backstage and introduced himself to the duo's drummer, who was a man by the name of Michael Bentine. Creative lunacy quickly began to spark between them over their ensuing chat and friendship, and as soon as Sellers became part of their equation it was clear that his sense of humour was operating on the same wavelength as theirs. In the late 1970s, Sellers recalled what the two of them were like in those days.

'Harry could belt out an aria and put even the greatest of opera singers to shame in a matter of seconds, but this relatively serious side to him was all a wonderful facade. The heart of a true loony was beating beneath that musical Welsh exterior. His act used to consist of him quite literally demonstrating the different ways that people shaved to the audience, and he'd do this with great speed and a manic smile on his face. He'd finish off by singing 'Falling In Love With Love', and I've heard stories that whenever he forgot the words, he'd get out of it by blowing the fruitiest raspberry that he could muster at the stalls.

'Mike was half of a musical double act called Sherwood and Forest, and his frizzy hair and beard looked as though there was enough voltage going through them to power the national gird. To this day I can remember the completely mind-boggled expressions of some of the audiences as he stood on stage spinning an epic yarn, using a broken old chairback as every single prop that cropped up during the course of his tale. They just didn't know what had hit them, because they were so used to comedians just standing there with the old 'I say, I say, I say . . .' and 'Take my wife . . . please' routines. This was like a

Frizzy-haired Mike Bentine and true-loony Harry Secombe.

bolt out of the blue, and as you can probably imagine, strange things would happen when the three of us got together.

'It was not unknown for Harry, Mike and myself to go into a tea room pretending to be high-ranking KGB spies. Strangled make-believe Russian accents could be heard alongside our frantic miming which implied that we were planning to make a bomb. Sometimes, it could clear a shop in minutes, but Mike came a cropper with that trick once when he was out with Harry. He tried to order some drinks using his cod-Slavic and it turned out that the waiter he was talking to was Hungarian, so he rumbled him in an instant . . .'

During this time, Secombe was appearing in a revue at the Hackney Empire, and when he and Bentine met up with Sellers in the theatre's bar after the show, they took the opportunity to introduce him to a fellow member of the audience whose spiralling flights of humorous fancy were equal to if not more bizarre than their own. Former Lance Sergeant Milligan, Terence A., had been posted in Tunisia for part of the duration of the war, where, as Sellers later explained, 'He nearly squashed Harry with a damn great howitzer as they were testing its firing mechanism on a plateau they'd positioned it on. The thing was that it wasn't actually as secure as they thought, so as it fired it took off like a rocket and crashed down a hundred feet below, right next to a wireless truck at the foot of the slope that Secombe was sitting in. The first thing that Harry knew about what had actually happened was when Spike poked his head through the canvas flaps at the back of the truck and said, "Anybody seen a gun?"

'I think it's safe to say that I certainly came across Harry and Mike prior to meeting Spike. He was pulling pints behind the bar at Jimmy Grafton's pub to help make ends meet, and living in the major's attic with an army of dusty spiders and a battered old typewriter which looked like something from the Stone Age . . .' Introducing Milligan,

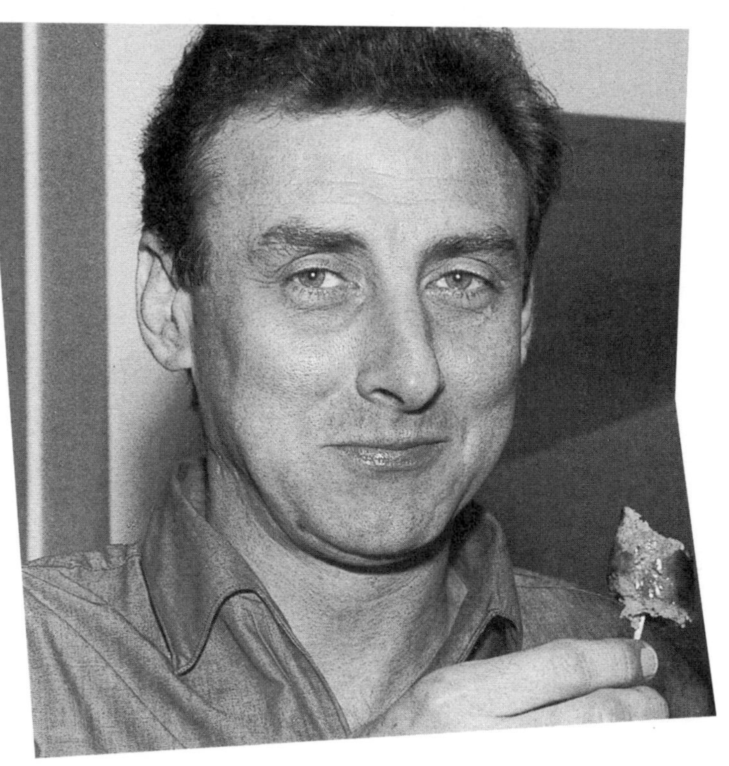

Former Lance Sergeant Milligan, Terence A. armed with a sausage.

The Goons, skippered by Spike, form up against Cambridge University for a Tiddly Winks match.

Secombe said to Sellers: *'You'll like Spike – the only trouble is, he is quite mad.'* Asked years later what had first intrigued him about Spike Milligan, Sellers replied: *'His name.'*

In order to be able to support both his wife and his two young children, along with his habit of writing comedy sketches and gags, Major James Grafton entered the family business after being demobbed and became the landlord of the Grafton Arms in Strutton Ground, near Westminster. His second cousin, Derek Roy, was one of the resident comedians on *Variety Bandbox* throughout the late

The Goons chew over their scripts.

1940s, so with that helpful connection material was quickly being typed up and broadcast.

As his connections grew, other writers and comedians began to hear how one of their number had a sideline as a publican, and as more and more of their numbers began to frequent his establishment so business began to boom. Bentine was introduced to Grafton through a mutual friend, and when Secombe asked for his advice over who to approach for new routines, he took him to see the major. Milligan moved into the attic, which you could only gain access to via a ladder, during early 1949 when he was also writing gags for Derek

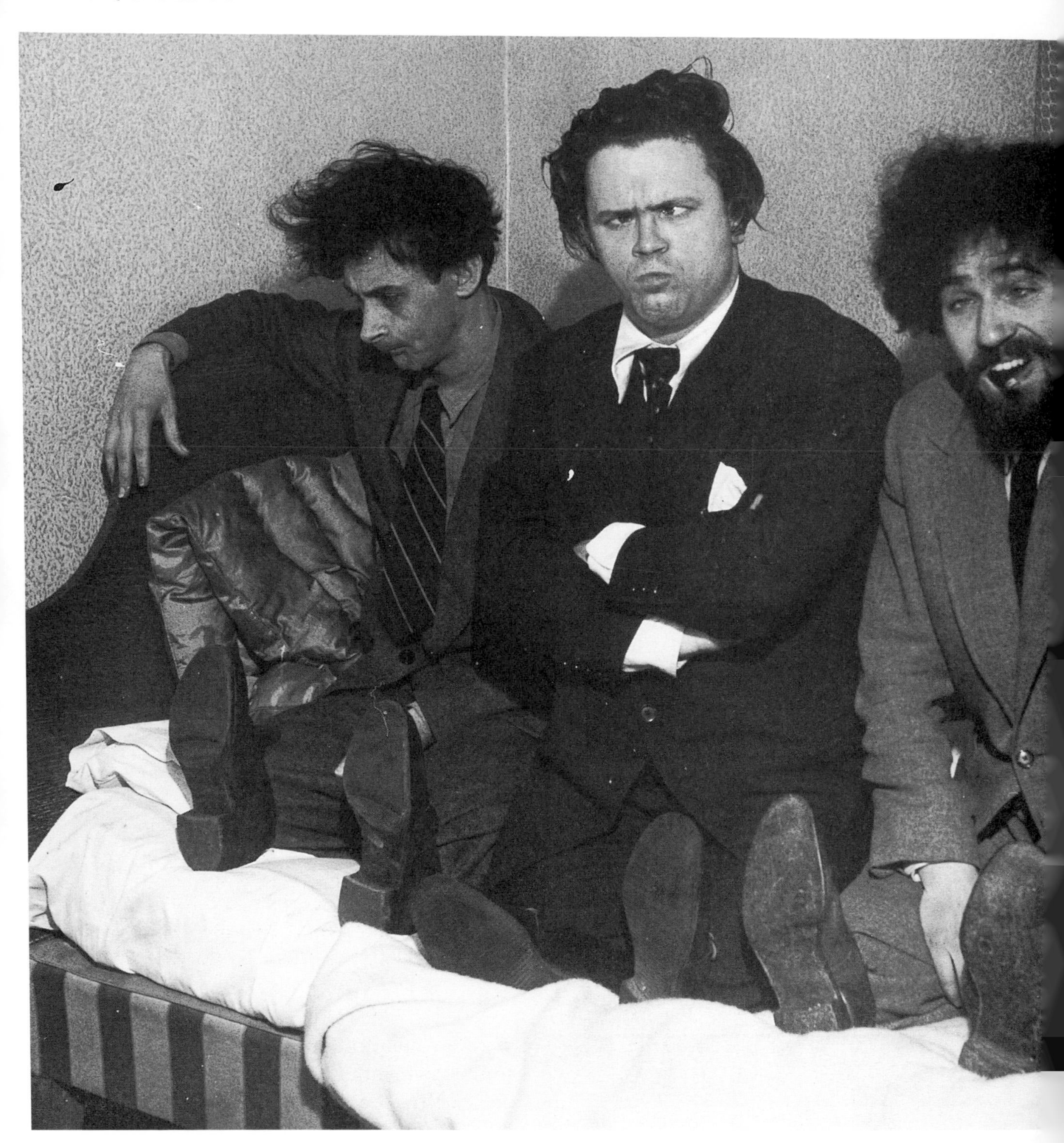

An ideas meeting in the production office.

Roy as well as material for Alfred Marks. He was soon collaborating with Grafton on scripts for *Hip, Hip Ho-Roy*, a radio vehicle for a certain relative of the major's.

United by circumstances and their anarchic sense of humour, Sellers, Milligan, Secombe and Bentine began spending an increasing amount of time together. Sellers and Milligan, in particular, got along famously and set about inflicting their brand of mayhem on to the unsuspecting people of London. Once the pair travelled on a bus pretending to be Germans. When the conductor asked for the fares, Milligan suddenly produced a phone from a cardboard box and started speaking into the receiver. 'Hello. Is zat zer German Embassy? Vere are ve going?' He then hung up and told Sellers: 'Dusseldorf'. When the puzzled conductor tried to explain that the bus was only going as far as Wood Green, Sellers leapt opposed to their nonsensical logic. But the show went from strength to strength and Sellers' ability to switch rapidly between Bloodnok, Bluebottle, Grytpype-Thynne and Henry Crun made him irreplaceable. Secombe admitted: 'If Spike was ill, Peter and I would take his place and if I was ill, Peter and Spike would take my place. But if Peter was ill, there was no show.'

Sellers always remembered *The Goon Show* with great affection. 'They really were my happiest days. I never had such fun, enjoyment or fulfilment either before or since. We were young men with very strong and ambitious ideas. There used to be a form of euphoria and we were

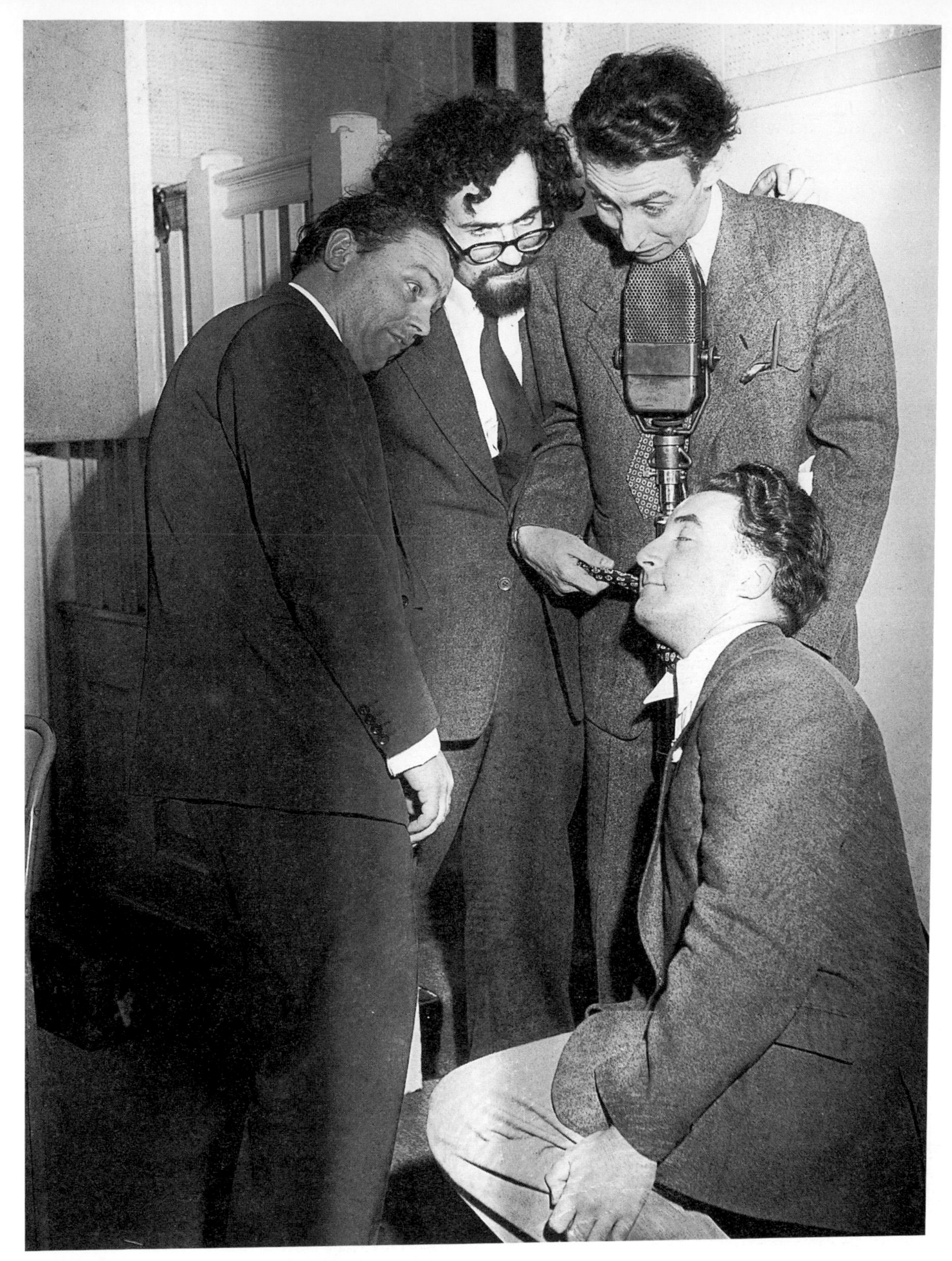

'Please assemble around the microphone'.

swept along and we swept people along with us. We were in another world.

'The show was, for us, an enormous release and we used to pack in so much energy. And all our ideas and thoughts went into the show; everything we had – we were just so keen to let people hear what was going on in our minds – this crazy, strange fantasy. I remember when we first met up, we all had this feeling that we had to do something. We had this thing inside us. We wanted to express ourselves in a sort of surrealistic form. We thought in cartoons, we thought in blackouts, we thought in sketches, we thought of mad characters. We would take a situation, and instead of letting it end normally, twist it around. This grew and grew.

'We were pioneers. I mean, we changed the whole face of humour in Britain and most other places as well. Everything that followed was weaned on that. *Beyond the Fringe* and *That Was The Week That Was* were born out of that. And all of them followed, Monty Python etc. Everything

A happy Sellers on the verge of stardom with the Goons announces his engagement to Anne Howe.

stopped on a Thursday evening, when *The Goon Show* was broadcast. The whole country came to a grinding halt. The public identified themselves with the characters and situations, because to many of them they were more than just funny voices. They were caricatures of real people.

'But we caused the BBC a lot of aggravation. We used to arrive on a Sunday and be apoplectic. I mean, we couldn't get through it. Then we'd have a run-through for the producer and sound effects, and most of those sound effects were wrong. Spike would have made a serious request like "Grand piano being played at high speed at sea." They'd put it on and he'd say, "Jesus! You'll have to do better than that!" And they'd go off for the afternoon, getting something else to sound like a grand piano at sea.'

The year in which *The Goon Show* began, 1951, was a happy one for Sellers all round. In September he married Australian actress Anne Howe after a typically unconventional proposal. There was no Mediterranean backdrop or going down on one knee for Sellers – instead he locked his future bride in a cupboard and only let her out on condition that she promised never to look at another man. Presumably the vicar was exempt from this agreement.

With the success of the Goons came the demand for provincial stage shows. Sellers was not keen because 'you're usually telling jokes to a crowd of people with two-thousandths of an inch of forehead.' His act – a bizarre one at the best of times – did not

always appeal to a matinee audience of pensioners who had only come into the theatre to keep out of the cold. He would walk on carrying a huge prop – such as a rolled-up carpet – and then completely ignore it. The front row would look at their watches and long for the return of Vera Lynn or Charlie Chester, someone they could understand. As Sellers grew bored, he would become increasingly outrageous. In darkness on stage at the Chiswick Empire he once fired a revolver. True, it was loaded with blanks but it certainly startled the Women's Institute party in the one and nines.

At the Hippodrome, Wolverhampton, Sellers interrupted the harmonica solo of *Goon Show* regular Max Geldray by announcing that there was a fire drill taking place next door. For Sellers, it was one of the joys of being principally a radio star – few people knew what he looked like. 'They didn't always know when we were gagging and when we were serious,' he laughed. Geldray was horrified at the prospect of Sellers clearing the theatre with a fire drill and his worst fears were realised when Sellers reappeared on stage in helmet, boots and trailing a length of hose. As Geldray watched nonplussed, Sellers proceeded to give a lecture on fire safety, concluding: 'I would like to thank you all for your attention. It is such a pleasure to deliver the message of fire prevention in such a luxurious temple of the Arts.'

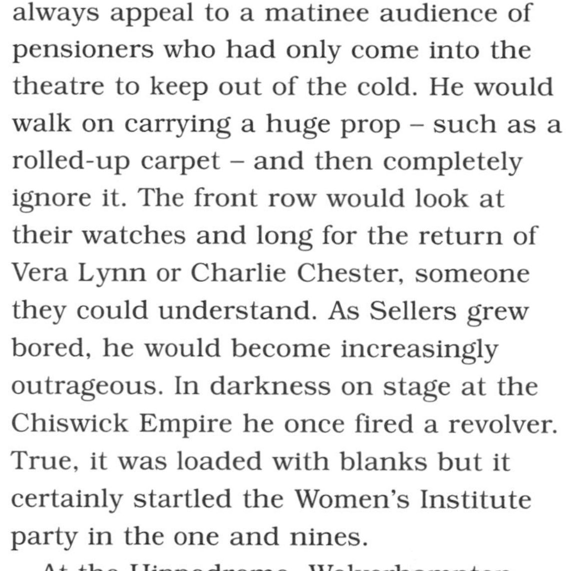

Two Goons go West.

He also managed to baffle a landlady or two in his time. When theatre work took him to Birmingham, he booked in to stay with a Mrs Reeve and arranged for her to take delivery of his prop basket in advance. The wicker hamper duly arrived but proved far too heavy for Mrs Reeve to shift single-handed. So she summoned her husband and son to help and together, they just about managed to carry it upstairs. No sooner had they gratefully put it down and started to gather their breath than the lid opened and out stepped Sellers with the words: 'Thank you – it's my legs, you know.'

The most notorious venue in the land was the Glasgow Empire where a net was usually draped across the stage to protect artists and the orchestra from flying glass. Only the brave, the foolish and the heavily-contracted played the Glasgow Empire. Sellers and Milligan came into the last two categories. Milligan's solo show had ended in a fracas with an abusive drunken critic from the Glasgow Herald so when it was Sellers' turn, he asked whether anybody was present from that austere organ. When a reply of 'yes' was heard, Sellers went into the wings, returned with a gramophone and put on 'God Save the Queen'. He then quietly walked off the stage, hailed a taxi and fled back to London. He later remarked that it was 'the first time an Englishman had left a Scottish audience standing.'

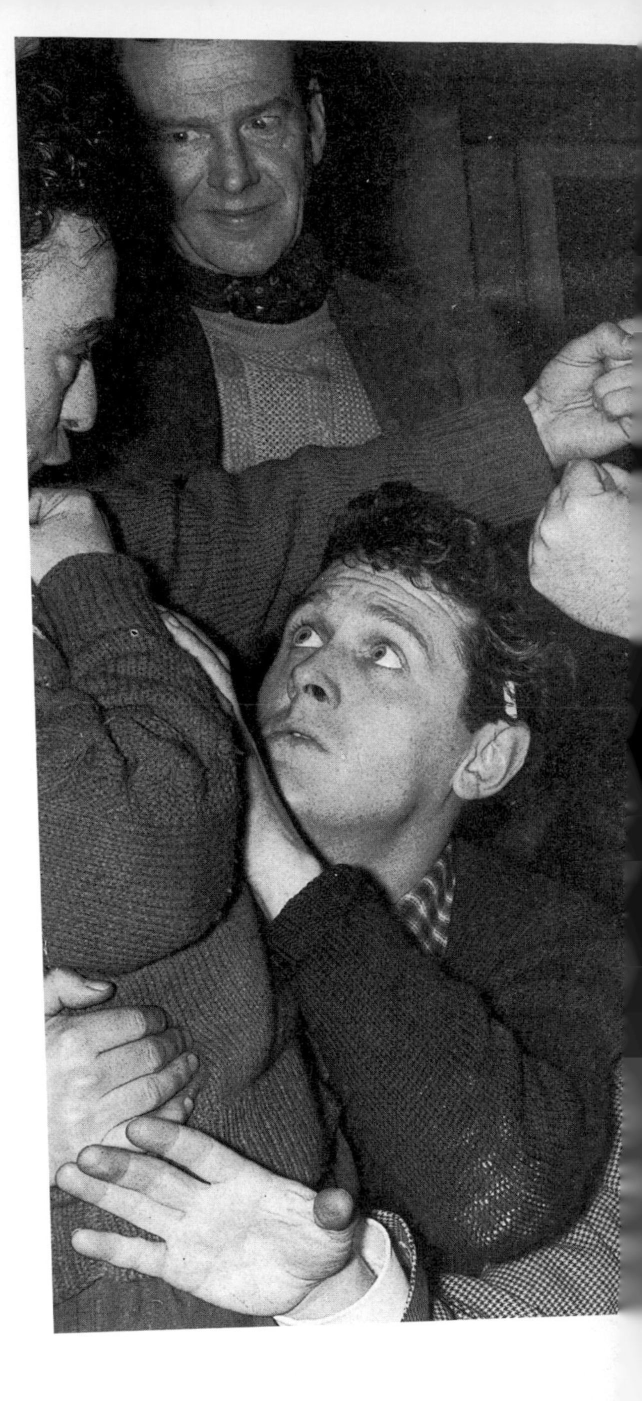

But his finest hour was one Christmas at the Coventry Hippodrome. Despite Sellers dying twice nightly on the Monday and Tuesday, there was a full house for the Wednesday matinee. 'I went out and saw all these old biddies and thought, "Oh God, I can't take this." So I fixed up a record player with the public address system. LPs had just come out and I bought a 10 inch LP of Wally Stott's Christmas melodies. I went on stage and said, "Ladies and gentlemen, we are

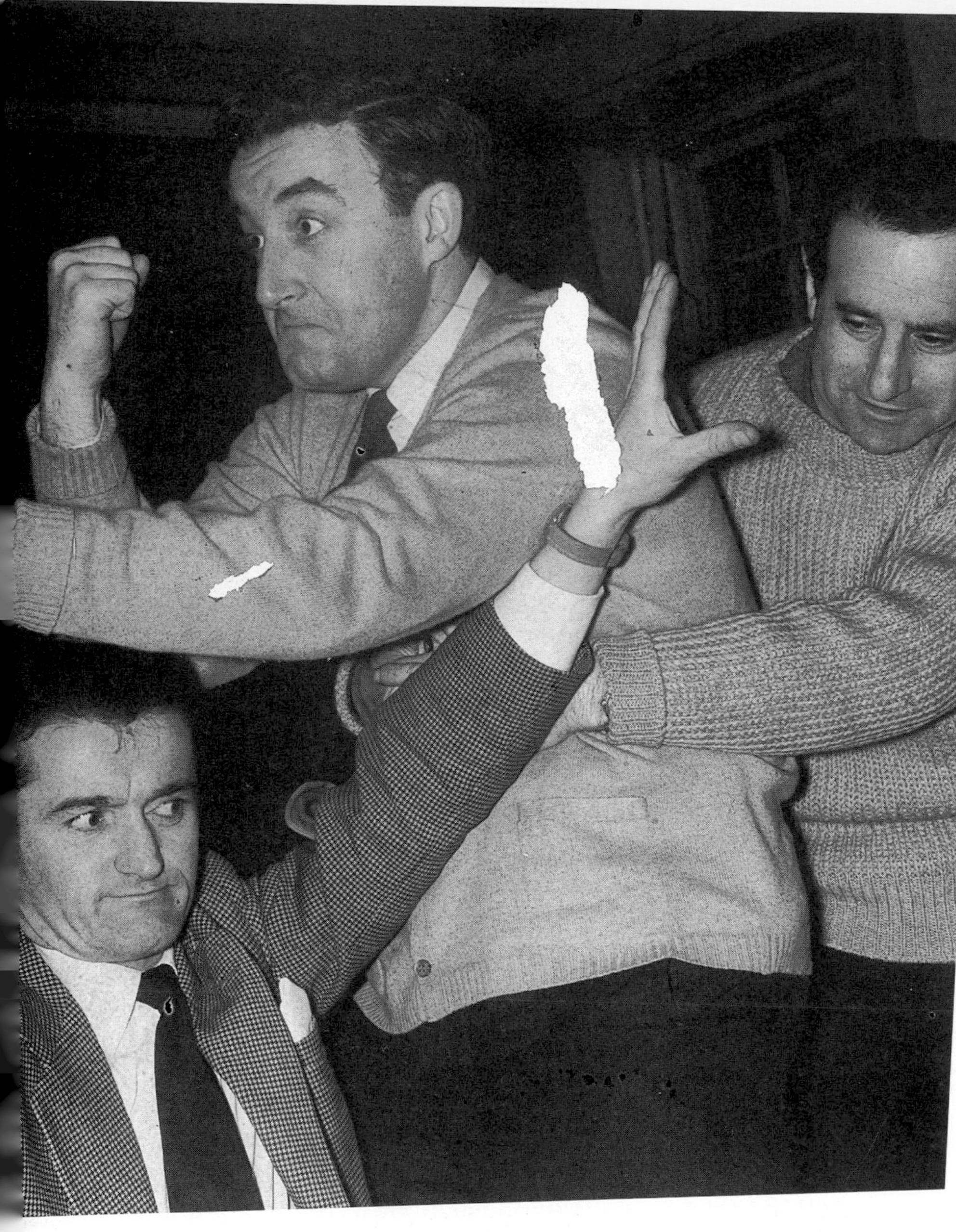

Rehearsing *The Idiot Weekly Price 2d.*

I think we can stand to hear that again – and all sing it together!" "Yes," they roared. My biggest mistake was ignoring the orchestra in the pit. They were sitting there, burning, through all this, and at the end they struck up 'Happy Days Are Here Again' in march tempo. When I got off stage, the manager let me have it. He said: "Your contract says you do your act as known. That is not as known.

nearing Christmas so I thought it would be nice if I played you some lovely Christmas songs on the gramophone to put us in a festive mood." I began with 'We Three Kings of Orient Are'. I looked at the record going round as if the audience weren't there. They cheered at the end so I put on 'Jingle Bells' and they went crazy. So I said, "Oh

You are not a gramophone player."'

A more rewarding venture was the expansion of the Goons into television with four series for the newly-created ITV – *The Idiot Weekly Price 2d*, *A Show Called Fred*, *Son of Fred* and *Yes, It's The Cathode Ray Tube Show* - the first three directed by the then unknown Richard Lester. At the time Sellers and Milligan had a thing about the name 'Fred'. 'We absolutely revered the name,' said Sellers. 'You can ruin anything with Fred. Suppose somebody shows you a painting. Oh, you say, that's beautiful. He says it's a Rembrandt. Beautiful, you say. Then you look a bit closer and you see it's signed 'Fred Rembrandt'. It's no good – you can't take it seriously if it's by someone called Fred. It's the epitome of working-class names.

'I think *Idiot Weekly* and *A Show Called Fred* were the best of the series. But it was a strain for Spike, writing a new show every week. Later on, we got together a group of young scriptwriters to contribute. They had some good ideas but sometimes there would be a good beginning but no end. In scriptwriting that isn't enough – the jokes have to be organised. That was when the show began to go downhill.'

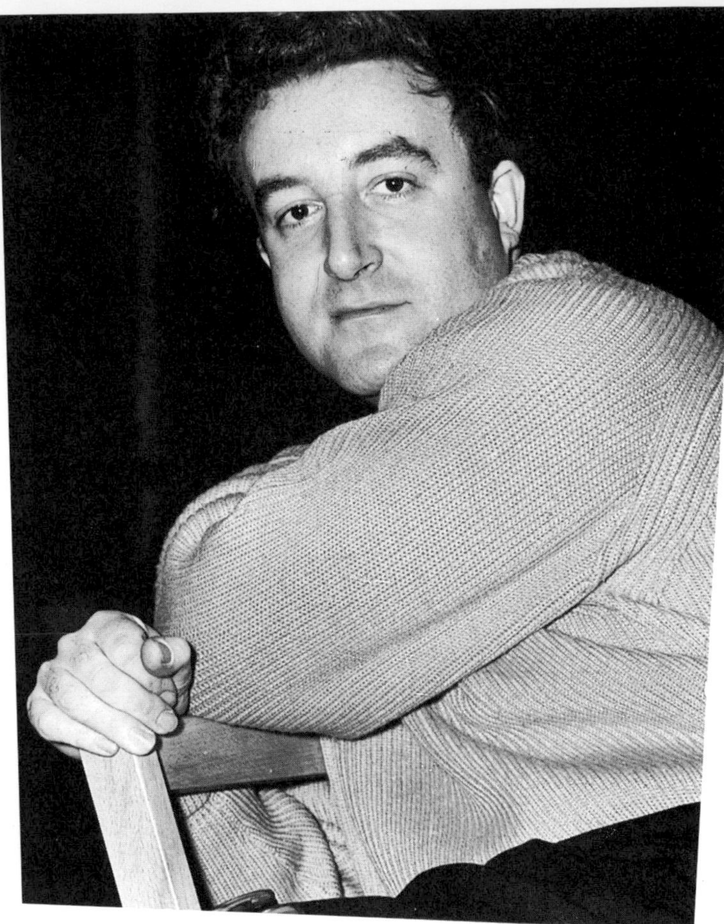

A less riotous moment on the set of *Idiot Weekly*.

Nevertheless Sellers found plenty to enjoy. One Milligan-penned sketch featured out-of-work actors deputising for zoo animals. Graham Stark donned a bathing costume in the sea lion pit and Kenneth Connor climbed in the monkeys' cage but what reduced Sellers to tears of laughter at the playback was the sight of Valentine Dyall, the sinister 'man in black', sidling up to a nervous-looking vulture. In another sketch, Sellers was supposed to be leading a dervish attack in the desert over a sand dune. The scene was filmed at a quarry near Harefield in the middle of summer but Sellers simply couldn't get a grip on the dry sand and kept sliding back down the dune. After his third attempt had ended in undignified failure, he started giggling to such an extent that he actually wet himself laughing. As he lay there helpless, a rivulet of urine trickled down the sand. He had to be taken home and shooting was abandoned for the day. It was an occupational hazard of filming with Peter Sellers.

Maurice Denham

Ubiquitous character actor Maurice Denham appeared in Two-Way Stretch with Sellers.

I remember Peter as a perfectionist. He was always working on ways to improve a scene, not just for himself but for others. All through *Two-Way Stretch* he was thinking up sight-gags - a funny walk, a prop - he had tremendous energy.

We were all friends on *Two-Way Stretch*. It was very relaxed and great fun to make. I remember quite a bit of giggling between Peter, David Lodge and Bernard Cribbins, and Wilfrid Hyde-White did a lot of laughing as well.

I remember I rang Peter up one day and a strange voice said 'Mr Sellers' residence.'

I thought it was Peter and said 'Come on, Peter, I know it's you!' The same voice said that he was Mr Sellers' butler and I still insisted it was Peter. It was just the sort of thing he did and he was very good with voices. Eventually the voice said he would fetch Mr Sellers and went off and Peter came on - I think it really was the butler.

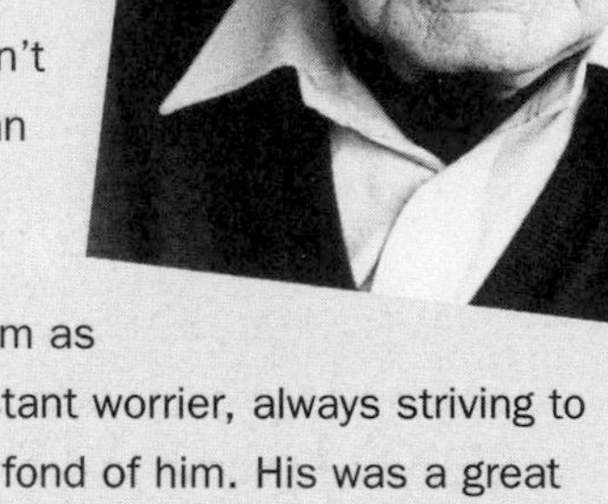

A few years after *Two-Way Stretch* I did a scene in *After the Fox*. Although Peter wasn't in this scene, we met and had lunch. Britt Ekland was there and Peter was his usual laughing self. Really when he wasn't acting he was just an ordinary bloke.

When I think of Peter I remember him as loveable and a constant worrier, always striving to improve. I was very fond of him. His was a great loss.

Mark Eden

Actor Mark Eden worked with Sellers in Heavens Above.

The word genius is bandied about a lot in this business but I think Peter was a genius. He was a brilliant mimic and he totally immersed himself in every role he played. He never played himself, even in real life. He was always doing different voices on the set of *Heavens Above*. I played Sir Jeffrey Despard in that film, and he was wonderful to work with. I remember there were a lot of kids in the cast and whenever they became fractious and bored waiting around on the set, Peter entertained them. He'd get out his ukulele and he'd do his George Formby for them. I thought for such a big star that was wonderful.

Sellers, with wife Britt Ekland at his side, places his handprint in cement at Grauman's Chinese Theatre, Hollywood.

Chapter 4

Bluebottle goes to Hollywood

'I was paid £20 for Let's Go Crazy. *It was shot in a basement in Wardour Street in just one room with an overhead light, and I played four different parts. I was desperate to get to Hollywood.'*
Peter Sellers interview, *The Daily Mail*, 1960

It was inevitable that Sellers would move into films sooner or later. His talent was such that he could command any medium but, as we have seen, he professed to having little love for the theatre, comparing it to a treadmill with night after night playing the same role. 'I'm an old movie buff,' he confessed. 'I can talk about all the old movies and even the new ones as well. And I wanted to be a movie actor, mainly because I knew that in the future I couldn't survive very well on repetition. Whenever I go to America, I carry an autograph book around with me, and I never say "It's not for me, it's for my sister" you know. I always say "It's for me – would you sign there?" Like when I first met Walter Pidgeon, or William Powell, and I thought, "Oh God Almighty – William Powell!" I'd sat there and watched him for years and I mean, it's ridiculous to ask for an autograph, except that you feel you're compelled to. You want to.'

Although his roots were in comedy, Sellers wanted to be treated as a serious actor. To this end, he had a picture taken in sombre mood and distributed to agents. A keen photographer, he actually took the portrait himself by setting up the camera and then striking a suitable pose. His early films such as *Let's Go Crazy* and *Down Among the Z Men* (*The Goon Show*'s only celluloid appearance) were strictly low-budget affairs and did little to project his image. In fact he found that he was in greater demand as a voice-over than as an actor. His genius for mimicry enabled him to play the voice of a cockatoo in the Joan Collins film *Our Girl Friday* and he also dubbed seventeen different voices – including eleven talking simultaneously in one scene – for Mike Frankovich's thriller *Malaga*.

Sellers as greasy-haired henchman Harry in *The Ladykillers.*

After bit parts as an army private in *Orders Are Orders* and as a policeman in John and Julie, his first big break came in 1956 with a major role in Ealing Studios' latest comedy *The Ladykillers*, starring Alec Guinness. Sellers himself later described it as his 'first real film'. Ealing and Guinness had already forged a formidable box-office partnership with *Kind Hearts and Coronets* (1949) and *The Lavender Hill Mob* (1951) so any collaboration was eagerly anticipated. At auditions for *The Ladykillers*, Sellers originally went up for the role of the hard-of-thinking ex-boxer One-Round (eventually played by Danny Green) but didn't look right for the part so he was cast instead as Harry, the greasy-haired henchman, on the strength of his ability to do an authentic teddy boy voice. For Sellers, working with Guinness presented an opportunity to watch the master in action. Sellers had long admired Guinness's virtuosity at playing multiple parts and set about studying him at close quarters. He admitted subsequently that he was 'emerald with envy' at the voice which Guinness had chosen for criminal mastermind Professor Marcus.

Right from the first day on set when Sellers did an impression of Guinness to his face and received an appreciative laugh, the two men got along famously. Sellers was deeply moved when learning that Guinness had written to a noted film critic: 'If you want a tip for the future, put your money on Peter Sellers.'

Another to be greatly impressed by Sellers' work was the film's producer Michael Balcon who, in 1960, recalled a remarkable spoof trailer which Sellers had made for *The Ladykillers.* 'One day,' said Balcon, 'we were all sitting in the studio canteen when over the loudspeaker came what sounded like the soundtrack from the film. But it wasn't the soundtrack. It was Peter impersonating all the actors himself on a tape recorder, including the camera director's remarks as well. People still talk about it in the studio – we were quite shaken.'

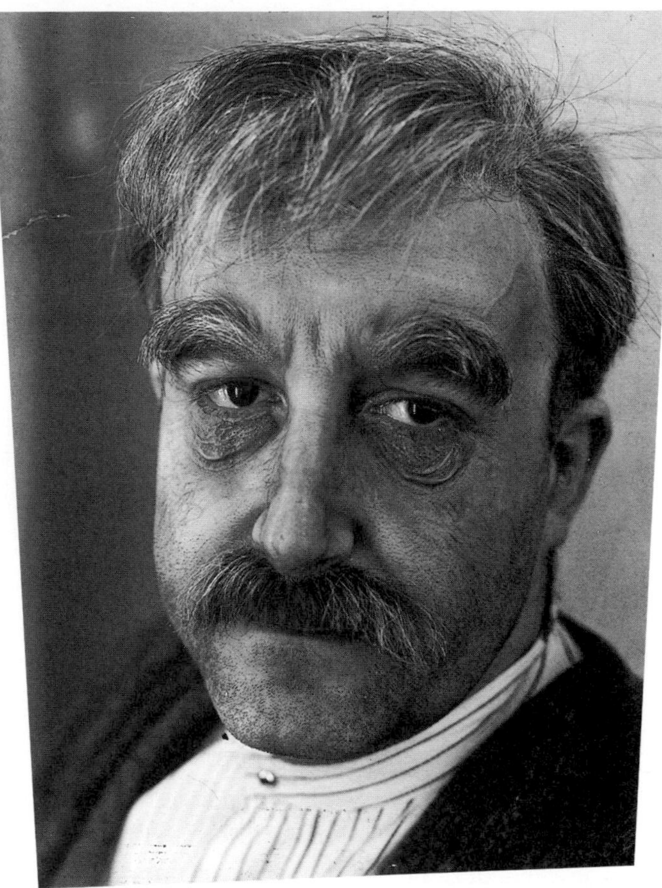

Percy Quill.

The Ladykillers also marked the beginning of an association with Herbert Lom who recalled a typical actors' prank from the film. 'Peter turned up on set in a big flash car so I and some others decided to borrow some washable paint and painted a big long scratch along one side. When he saw it, Peter nearly fainted. A few days later, I was driving home in my car when I noticed an unpleasant smell coming from the engine. I stopped the car, looked under the bonnet and found a kipper. In revenge, Peter had pinned the kipper at the bottom of the engine of my car and it had started frying whenever the engine got hot!'

Impressed by his portrayal of the ancient William Mate Cobblers on *Idiot Weekly*, producer Michael Relph cast Sellers as 68-year-old projectionist Percy Quill in *The Smallest Show on Earth*, the tale of the crumbling Bijou Kinema. Incidentally, Cobblers, like most of Sellers' creations, was based on a real person. 'He's got a furniture shop near Spike's office,' said Sellers in 1958. 'You go in and say "What sort of wood is this?"

And he says "Solid wood, that is."

Sellers' reputation as the 'man of a thousand voices' plus his knack of slipping in and out of a whole range of characters was further enhanced with his first starring role in *The Naked Truth*, the title of a fictional tabloid newspaper. He played Sonny MacGregor, Scottish TV host and master of disguise whose alter-egos included an old seadog, an Irish safecracker and an English country squire.

Ever keen to use new-fangled technology, Sellers would take to the streets of London armed with one of the earliest reel-to-reel tape recorders to study people's voices. 'Having worked in radio, the voice is always the starting point for me,' he explained. 'The voice tells me a lot about the character, so I can start to see it and fill it out. I would go down to a studio with some kind of an idea and ad-lib for about an hour with a tape recorder. Then I'd play it all back, choose what seemed to come off and work over that. After perfecting the character's voice, I begin to work on his look. Some actors work the other way round – they get the make-up first and fit the voice to it. I make a lot of drawings of him as I think he should look, then I get together with the make-up man and sort of transfer the drawings on to my face. Next I try to establish how he walks – very important, the walk. Finally in full make-up, I confront myself in the mirror. I stare at my image waiting for the man I'm going to portray to stare back at me. If I'm lucky, it happens. The character has taken over.'

The real Peter Sellers.

When *The Naked Truth* opened in London, among the audience was an aspiring young director named Joe McGrath. On his way out, he spotted Sellers lurking in the foyer, eavesdropping on the audience's verdict. McGrath walked over to him and said, in a manner mocking newspaper competitions of the time: 'You are the real Peter Sellers, and I claim the £10 prize!' Sellers liked McGrath's sense of humour and the pair became friends with McGrath going on to direct him in *Casino Royale, The Magic Christian* and *The Great McGonagall.* Any friend of Sellers soon came to realise that the only thing that was predictable about him was his unpredictability. McGrath remembered: 'I got a call from Peter once at four o'clock in the morning. I was in bed, picked the phone up and said, "Hello". The voice on the other end said, "Hello Joe, it's Pete here." I said, "God, Peter, what is it?" He said, "Where am I?" I said, "What's the number on your telephone?" He said, "It's zero, zero, four, five, three, two." I said, "You're at home." "Oh thank God for that," he said and hung up.'

With the help of his agent, John Redway, Sellers came to the attention of the Boulting brothers, John and Roy, whose string of Fifties social comedy successes included *Private's Progress*, *Brothers in Law* and *Lucky Jim*. Redway phoned John Boulting and asked him to watch Sellers in a TV sketch that evening in which Sellers was playing a sarcastic schoolmaster. Boulting was impressed. He said of Sellers' performance: 'He looked ordinary enough, but the way he played – acid-tongued, very incisive, was brilliant. No need of a funny voice either. As I recall, his voice sounded rather like Alec Guinness's.'

The Boultings wasted no time in signing Sellers to a £100,000 non-exclusive, five-year contract and he made his debut for them supporting Terry-Thomas in *Carlton-*

Ian Bannen as the King of Gallardia with Sellers as Amphibulos in *Carlton-Browne of the F.O.*

Liza Minelli frequently visited Sellers on the set of another Boulting Brothers' comedy, *Soft Beds, Hard Battles.*

Browne of the F.O., a satire about British foreign diplomacy. Sellers struggled at first to find a voice for Amphibulos, prime minister on the Mediterranean island of Gaillardia, until Roy Boulting did an impression of Italian film entrepreneur Filippo del Guidice on whom the character had been roughly based. Boulting said: 'Within two minutes, Peter proceeded to improvise dialogue and put on an act as a man he'd never seen which was more 'Del' than Del himself.'

Early in 1958, Sellers made a surprise return to the stage at the request of producer Peter Hall who, absorbed by his performance in *The Naked Truth*, wanted him to play a devious Arab potentate in the West End comedy *Brouhaha*. It was to be an experience which neither Sellers – nor any of his co-stars – would ever forget.

It all started well enough but then Sellers, bored with repeating the same routine, began improvising - firstly with dialogue, then costumes and entrances. It would have come as little surprise if he had suddenly switched theatres half-way through. He explained: 'The first act was very good, the last act wasn't too bad, but it really took a dive in the middle – and I was determined to try and beat this. In those days it was taboo to do any improvisation but we'd worked out all kinds of things to do – or at least I had with some of the actors who I knew I could sling lines at and who wouldn't suddenly freeze in the corner. One day we were on and I said to Leo McKern: "Why

At rehearsals for *Brouhaha*

don't we do a balancing act in the middle of this scene, like they do in variety?" He said, "What a good idea" and I said, "Because I've just come off the stage and it's like playing to Hell out there – teacups rattling, old people dying.'"

Perhaps understandably, not all of his co-stars were as amenable to sudden re-writes as McKern. Some actually liked to have a vague idea of what they would be doing when they stepped out on stage and voiced their disapproval accordingly. 'I was given the sack I don't know how many times,' confessed Sellers.

Sellers played three roles in *The Mouse That Roared*:
A Prime Minister (above), a Field Marshal and. . .

To add to his burden, Sellers' theatre run coincided with the daytime shooting of his latest film, *The Mouse That Roared.* Matters came to a head one evening when he arrived at the theatre decidedly the worse for wear after attending a party in honour of the newly-knighted Alec Guinness. Then followed the famous incident recounted earlier by Dennis Selinger, when half-way through the performance, he announced to the audience that he was 'sloshed' – 'a confession which was all too superfluous' he admitted later - and suggested that his understudy be brought on to replace him. He called for a show of hands as to whether he should step down but the audience wouldn't hear of such a thing and voted overwhelmingly for him to carry on. Their faith was to be wholly justified as comedy turned into pure farce. For when it came to the scene where he danced with Hermione Harvey, Sellers made her dance the wrong way round, tripped over something, fell into the pit and dragged her down there with him! Looking back on the incident, he said: 'I took two or three steps too many towards the footlights – and I just went straight over, with her as well, and how we managed to miss a pile of old iron down there. . . We dropped literally 8ft from a standing position into the pit, with her on top of me. Wham! It was an enormous laugh. They must've thought there were mattresses down there and we did this every night.' His left leg had to be bandaged as a result of the fall but although an ambulance was called, he refused to go to hospital. Not surprisingly, his run in *Brouhaha* ended shortly afterwards.

In the same year Sellers also succeeded in upsetting the BBC. Filling in a few moments at the end of a live programme, *The April 8th Show,* he decided to spice things up in his own Goonish manner by tearing up the roller caption and crying, 'It's all lies! It's all been Tom Sloan's

. . . Grand Duchess Gloriana XII

fault, him and his liniment.' (Sloan was the Assistant Head of Light Entertainment and Sloan's Liniment was a make of embrocation). To Sellers, it was just a joke but the BBC took a dim view of such sacrilegious treatment of its property and for a while Sellers became *persona non gratis.*

The Corporation's attitude was not mirrored by film producers and Sellers' second collaboration with the Boulting Brothers brought him the role which he described as 'undoubtedly the turning point in my career'. The film was *I'm All Right, Jack,* a sequel to the Boultings' *Private's Progress* following the fortunes of that innocent at large Stanley Windrush (played by Ian Carmichael). In *I'm All Right, Jack,* Windrush has landed a job as a forklift operator at Missiles Ltd, the factory owned by his unscrupulous Uncle Bertie (Dennis Price), and where the shop steward is the Marxist Fred Kite. The role of Kite was to be the making of Peter Sellers.

'From a sort of screen odd-job man and general impersonator, I was suddenly lifted by this film into a world of stardom. And I had got the part quite casually, as the result of a chat at a charity cricket match. I was playing for John Boulting's team in a game at Totteridge and after the match he mentioned that he had a part in a film he was preparing which he thought would suit me. The part intrigued me particularly because there

Sellers in the role of Fred Kite - a turning point in his career

had been a lot of strikes recently and the TV news had been full of fascinating interviews with stony-faced strike leaders saying things like "My politics is a secret between me and the ballot-box."'

In spite of his apparent enthusiasm, Sellers turned down the script when he first read it because he didn't think Kite's part was funny enough. John Boulting, knowing that Sellers was never happy until he had 'found' a character's voice, suggested that Sellers make a short screen test. Sellers agreed and set about creating the look of Fred Kite. First he went to a leading London tailor's and came back with an ill-fitting suit before heading off to the barber's for a severe haircut – 'Gestapo short' as he called it. Then he came up with the idea of giving Kite a Hitler moustache. When he finally looked in the mirror as Fred Kite, he didn't recognise himself – and that was exactly the way he liked it.

There was still the matter of the voice which he acquired from watching television clips of union delegates coming and going from Downing Street. He was particularly enthralled by their clipped tones and highly individual command of the English language. 'Reporters would hold up microphones and these fellows would say: "The situation, as I see it, is that the negotiations have reached a point of stagnation and all that can happen now is that they will reverberate to the detriment of the masses. All I am prepared to say at this juncture is that my colleagues and I are going to withdraw and consult." He took Kite's malapropisms and mispronunciations from one of the film crew, a chief grip, who, when Sellers tripped over a cable, asked: 'Can I assist you in your predicalament?'

'I had a bit of luck with the character,' admitted Sellers. 'There was a trades union official I used to know at one of the studios. He was the type who always had about six pencils in his breast pocket. Or else he used to rush about with a little notice board in his hands and a list of names on a sheet of paper fastened on with paper clips. I'm sure it was completely useless. But I was able to draw on him for aspects of the character too.'

Sellers did the screen test to spontaneous applause from the crew, perhaps partly because they all recognised colleagues. 'After that, I really did live the part and with that haircut and moustache, I rarely went out. To me, Fred Kite was a tragic figure, a man of great authority at the factory but a henpecked mess in his own home.'

I'm All Right, Jack won Sellers a BAFTA Award for Best Actor. It is also said to have assisted the Conservative Party to

Sellers' next film was *Two-Way Stretch* - the story of three convicts who plan to use their presence in prison as an alibi for a diamond robbery.

win the 1959 general election. 'I think it probably helped a bit,' concluded Sellers. 'I heard the Tories liked it. It probably did more good to them than it did to Labour.'

The films were coming thick and fast now – *Two-Way Stretch, The Battle of the Sexes* and *Never Let Go* were all released in the first six months of 1960. Once again, they illustrated Sellers' outstanding versatility, as he moved effortlessly from crafty Cockney convict Dodger Lane in *Two-Way Stretch* to quiet

Dodger Lane - unrepentant law breaker.

Scottish accountant Mr Martin in *The Battle of the Sexes* and on to his first serious dramatic role as gangster Lionel Meadows in *Never Let Go.* Although he was now established as a major star courted by Hollywood, Sellers never forgot his old mates like Graham Stark and David Lodge. Sellers' influence is thought to have helped Lodge, a fine comedy actor in his own right, land a small part in *I'm All Right, Jack* and the role of incompetent safecracker Jelly Knight in *Two-Way Stretch.* Stark and Lodge also joined Sellers in *The Running, Jumping and Standing Still Film,* eleven minutes of barely-controlled madness shot on a budget of £700 in two days with Sellers' new camera and showing a distinguished cast romping around in a London field. Only the men in white coats were missing. The film did well enough to earn an Oscar nomination and became such a firm favourite of Princess Margaret and Lord Snowdon that Sellers gave them a print of the film. The royals in turn agreed to appear in one of Sellers' home movies where Lord Snowdon played a gangster before teaming up with Princess Margaret and Sellers for a glorious chorus line finale of the *Gang Show* classic 'Riding Along on the Crest of a Wave' (Sellers still had a thing about Ralph Reader).

Quiet Scottish accountant Mr Martin.

For the immediate future, however, it was not Princess Margaret but another of the world's most famous women whose name would be inextricably linked to that

With friend and fan Princess Margaret.

of Peter Sellers. He had said that he wanted 'to become so successful that I can name the parts I want and play them the way I want' and his wish was granted when he was chosen to star opposite the glamorous Sophia Loren in *The Millionairess.* Sellers was in awe from day one. 'I don't normally act with romantic, glamorous women,' he told reporters, adding somewhat unnecessarily: 'She's a lot different from Harry Secombe.'

Afterwards he reflected: 'This was my first really big international film and Sophia Loren was the biggest star I'd been cast with. I was genuinely scared – overwhelmed. I said to her, "After all those marvellous men you've acted with – people like William Holden and Charlton Heston – I must seem almost insignificant." Being in that film with her helped to change my brand image. Before that I'd never got any heart-throb fan mail. But after being with Sophia and winning her in the film, it all changed. Mail began to come in from women. It was as though they'd decided that if I was good enough for Sophia, I was good enough for them too.'

Sellers was also initially wary of Alastair Sim, who played a crooked lawyer in *The Millionairess,* until Sim admitted that he was a great fan of *The Goon Show.* As shooting progressed, Sellers became increasingly enchanted by Loren, not least because she laughed at his jokes. He and Graham Stark, who was playing a butler, conspired to teach Loren Cockney rhyming slang. One morning she went up to director Anthony Asquith, looked him in the eyes and said: 'Ow you like a bunch of fives right up the froat?'

After *The Millionairess,* Sellers was perceived as a sex symbol and cast in more romantic roles; here he plays opposite glamorous Mai Zetterling as her lover in *That Uncertain Feeling.*

Sellers poses with his co-star to-be Sophia Loren, before shooting begins on *The Millionairess*.

In character, Sellers and Loren even made a record together – 'Goodness Gracious Me' – which, although not in the film, reached number four in the UK charts. They followed it up fourteen months later with another hit, 'Bangers and Mash', possibly the only song in history devoted to the virtues of mashed potato. Sellers changed the doctor in *The Millionairess* from an Arab to an Indian because, ever since spending time in India during the war, he had appreciated the comic potential of that country's accent. He and Milligan had perfected the Indian accent in the Goons with characters Singhiz Lalkaka Thingz (Sellers) and Babu Banajee (Milligan). 'They became incredibly popular those two,' Sellers told Michael Parkinson in 1974, 'and all kinds of things happened after that. I was invited to speak at the Oxford Union's Indian Society once, and a very kind gentleman introduced me and said that it was due to me that members of the Indian race were allowed to get past the garden fence with their carpets because people sounded like Spike and I.'

Sellers stated that he felt the character of Dr Kabir had taken him over during the making of the film. 'I felt I had actually been an Indian in some past life. Once during filming, an Indian supporting player came up to me and said, without joking, that I was the new messiah and ought to go to India and lead her people into a happier future. I even began to feel I had developed the power to heal people along with the role. It was frightening.' As with

Sellers as Dr Ahmed el Kabir in *The Millionairess.*

Sellers and Sophia Loren cause a diversion.

Fred Kite, Sellers lived the role off-set and began speaking in an Indian accent over dinner at home. Even years later when walking into an Indian restaurant, he would slip into an Indian accent. He just loved the sound of it.

The Millionairess propelled Sellers into the big league of earners, thereby enabling him to indulge in his passion for cars and cameras. In 1962, he calculated that he had owned sixty different cars since 1949, the rapid turnover prompting one car salesman in north London to open up a showroom entirely for the actor's benefit. 'I've lost money on every car but one,' admitted Sellers, 'and that was one I only kept for a few hours. It was a Vauxhall – that was my level in those days. I bought it in the morning and sold it by lunchtime. And I made £50 on the deal.' A less successful purchase was a magnificent Bentley Continental. On getting it home, Sellers discovered that it was too big to fit into his garage. So he had to have the garage demolished and a new one built.

The man given the task of keeping track of Sellers' motoring whims (which included a 12-seater bus and a few go-karts) was Tony Crook – an unfortunate name for a car dealer. Crook revealed how Sellers would often ring him from some foreign land having just seen a beautiful car flash by. He would describe

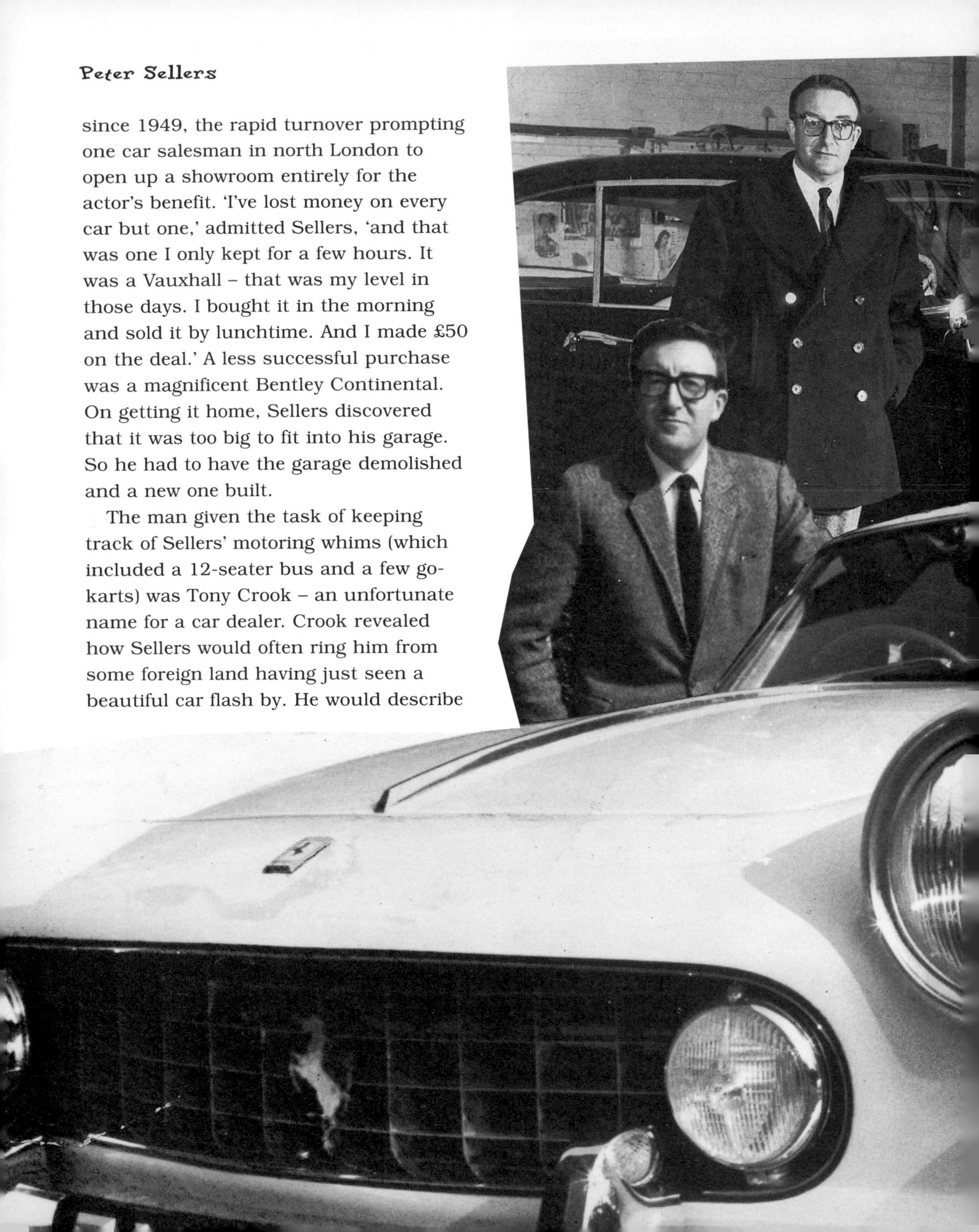

Car-mad Sellers with his Bentley – which he can only dream of taking out on the road - and with his fully road-worthy 150 m.p.h. Ferrari 250 GT.

the vehicle to Crook over the phone and then, if the price was right, ask him to buy one. 'Supplying Peter with cars was pretty well a full-time job,' confessed Crook.

Early in his career, cars were very nearly Sellers' downfall. At the wheel of his Triumph Gloria, he fell asleep, ran off the road through a thick hedge and ended up in a ploughed field. Lucky to escape with nothing more serious than a few bruises, he was still able to record that week's *Goon Show.*

Sellers' other great passion was photography.

He was equally mad about photography and would go to any lengths to buy the latest photographic equipment. Director Bryan Forbes remembers talking on the phone to Sellers from St. Moritz. 'I told him, "There's a camera shop here with some fabulous gear." Peter caught the next plane out from England!'

Sellers continued to draw inspiration for his film roles from people he had met or heard. 'I patterned the voice of the Welsh librarian in *Only Two Can Play* on a man Kenneth Griffith introduced me to in Swansea, I modelled Rev Smallwood in *Heavens Above!* on Brother Cornelius who taught me at St Aloysius College when I was eleven, and I based the voice of the old retired general in *Waltz of the Toreadors* on the Earl of Dudley whose parties I used to go to at his home in Hertfordshire. He threatened to sue if the film was no good! He lived near me and I remember meeting there Gary Cooper, a screen idol of mine, just before he died. I think I'd have been terribly disappointed if Cooper had not been as good a shot in real life as he was in the movies. We went shooting and he downed two birds, one with each barrel, while we were talking.'

Throughout his film career, Sellers made no secret of his dislike for Hollywood executives, a loathing which dated back to his first trip to Tinseltown when he overheard a minion refer to him as 'the property'. Nevertheless one of his most enjoyable experiences was

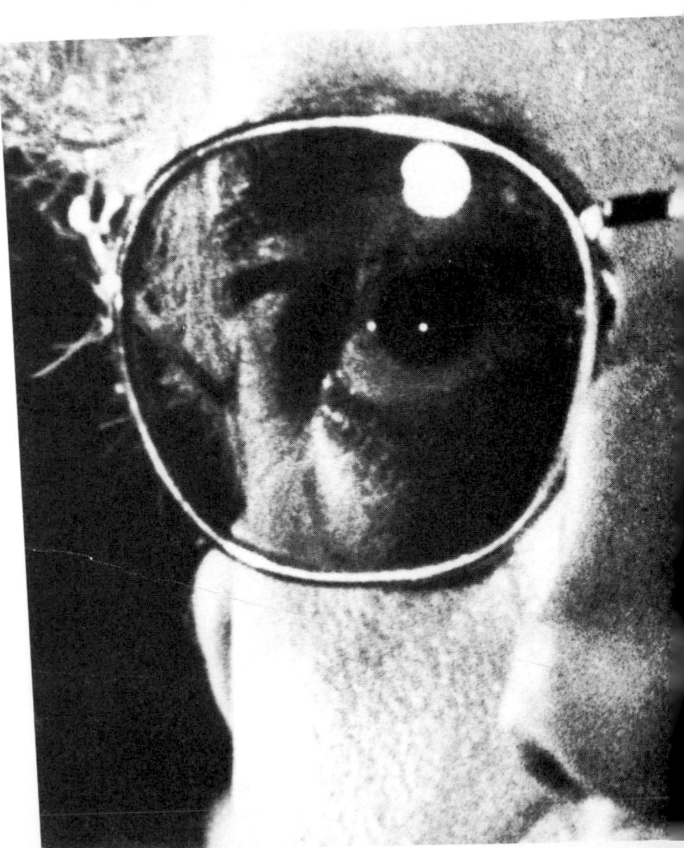

filming *Lolita* with rising director Stanley Kubrick. Having said that, Kubrick had to work hard to persuade Sellers to take on the chameleon-like Clare Quilty, by far his most controversial role to date. Kubrick knew that the key to unlocking Sellers' reluctance was for him to 'find' Quilty's voice. 'Stanley wanted me to speak with a New York accent. He said, "Listen, a friend who's a jazz impresario, Norman Granz, has a really perfect sound." So he put this tape on, and it was hysterical. You heard a voice, speaking too loud, saying, with a lisp, "Hi there, Stanley, this is Norman. Jesus Christ, this is a whole script, for God's sakes. I mean, you really do ask for some strange things." Then you hear some rustling of paper, and he starts reading the *Lolita* script. And that's where Quilty came from.

'Quilty was a fantastic nightmarish character, part homosexual, part drug addict, part sadist, part masochist, part anything twisted and unhealthy you can think of. He had to be horrifying and at the same time funny. I had never met anyone at all like this so I just had to guess, to construct an imaginative idea for myself of what such a person must be like. When I saw myself on screen, I thought: "This time you've done it – no one will ever believe this." But then in the U.S. I actually ran into a couple of people

Sellers also starred in Kubrik's *Dr Strangelove: or, How I Learned to Stop Worrying about the Bomb* (above - on the set – and left).

who might almost have been role models for the character and I began to think: "Oh well, perhaps you weren't so far out after all."'

The success of *Lolita* in 1962 was tempered by the death of Sellers' father Bill from a heart attack at the age of 62. Sellers' marriage was also deteriorating fast but he threw himself into work, teaming up again with Bernard Cribbins and Lionel Jeffries for *The Wrong Arm of the Law*, a follow-up to *Two-Way Stretch*. It was very nearly his last film as he came within inches of being mown down by his old pal Graham Stark. Filming a scene at Elstree aerodrome, Stark, who had promised director Cliff Owen that he had experience of riding a motorcycle, was required to pilot a 500cc machine with Davy Kaye as his passenger. Owen told Stark that he wanted the bike to head straight for the camera before veering away at the last minute. Stark duly aimed the machine in the direction of the camera, near which Sellers happened to be sitting relaxing in a deckchair. All was going well until the throttle suddenly jammed. As Stark waved frantically, Sellers was roused spectacularly from his lethargy and let out an anguished cry as he leapt to safety seconds before the bike roared past,

Off the set of *The Wrong Arm of the Law*, Sellers talks to producer Aubrey Baring.

missing the chair by a matter of inches. A stunned Owen told Stark that he presumed his previous bike-riding experience had been on the Wall of Death.

Sellers regularly consulted psychic Maurice Woodruff to chart his career but even he could not have predicted the circumstances which would lead to him playing the inimitable Inspector Jacques Clouseau, pride of the French Sûreté. For Sellers only landed the role after Peter Ustinov, the first choice of writer/director Blake Edwards, had turned it down. Ustinov's loss was to be Sellers' gain.

Clouseau's impact on *The Pink Panther* was immediate. In his very first scene, he puts his hand on a spinning globe and falls flat on his face. Blake Edwards told the *New York Times* in 1978: 'When we got on the set, we had a sequence introducing the inspector. He was saying "We must find that woman." Looking at it, I didn't see that we were incorporating any physical humour and I felt that if

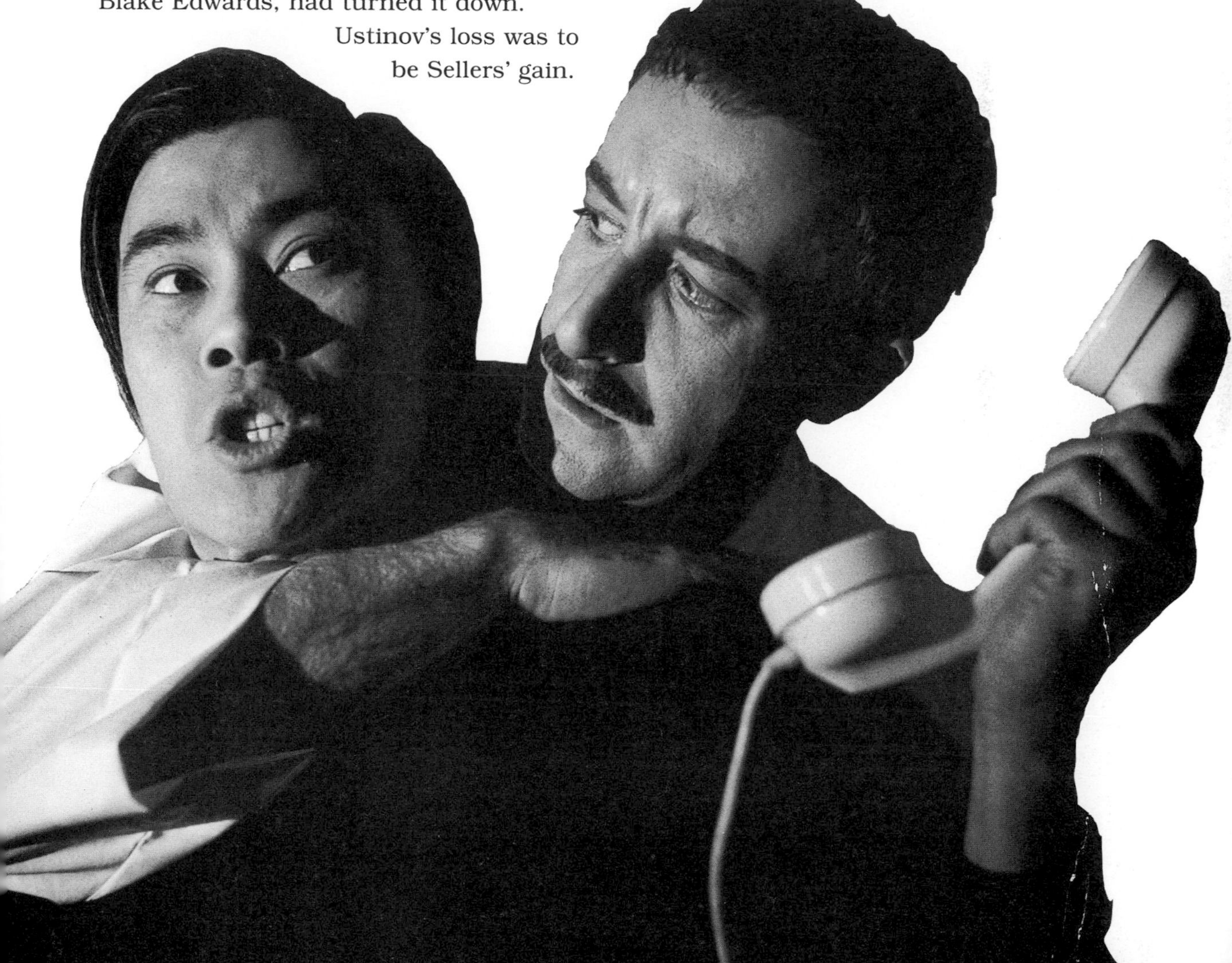

Clouseau locked in combat with faithful manservant Cato.

we're going to do it, we'd better do it in the first scene. I saw a giant globe on the set, so I suggested Peter spin the globe at first. After he made the declaration, "We must find that woman," he would lean on the globe and it would fling him out of the frame. The die was cast. Peter is not really a physical comedian in the sense that Chaplin or Keaton were; he is not that kind of an acrobat and he is not trained that way. But he has a mind that thinks that way.'

Sellers invented the look of Clouseau on the flight out to Rome prior to filming *The Pink Panther.* 'Suddenly something came to me – Captain Webb matches. That's an old British brand of safety matches. On its package is a guy in a long, straight, striped, old-fashioned bathing costume, with a big stiff moustache standing out on his face. I thought that one of the things some Frenchmen have is this ostentatious show of virility.

'I set out to play Clouseau with great dignity because I feel that he thinks he is probably one of the greatest detectives in

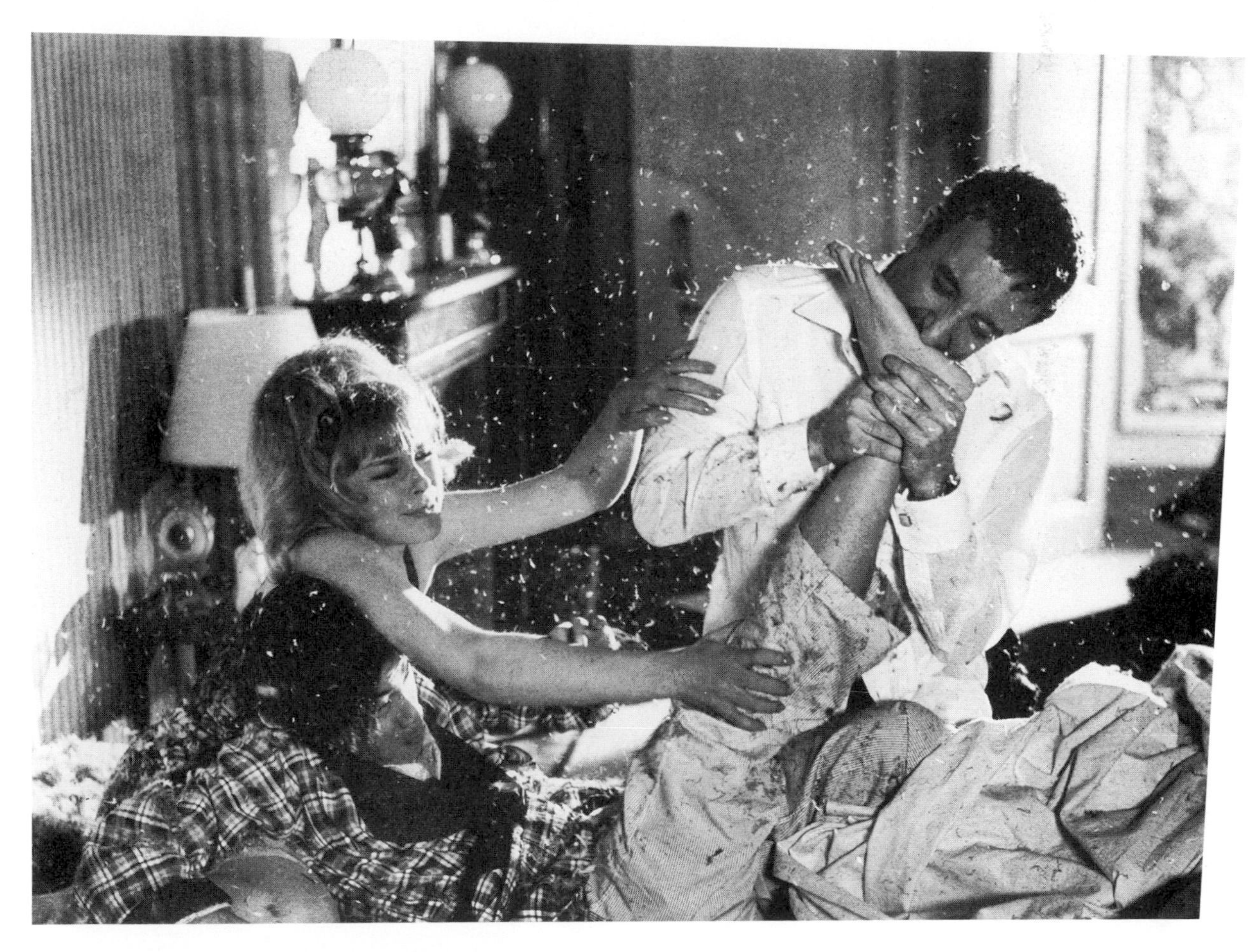

Cato intrudes on Inspector Clouseau's attempt at seduction.

THE MIRISCH CORPORATION presents

A BLAKE EDWARDS PRODUCTION

PETER SELLERS ELKE SOMMER

"Please Inspector, can't we settle this before we get to the Police Station?"

A SHOT IN THE DARK

COLOUR by DeLU

the world. The original script makes him out to be a complete idiot. I thought a forgivable vanity would humanise him and make him kind of touching. The clumsiness was part of what Blake wanted him to be. Because of this dignity, Blake wanted him to be, shall we say, accident-prone. That's why when

It's a struggle for Clouseau to maintain his dignity in this scene from *A Shot in the Dark.*

something happens to him, like he falls over something, he gets up from the floor and says to his assistant, who's been completely silent, "What was that you said?" The assistant says: "Nothing, sir." And he can only say: "Er, yes, I see." That's how his mind works. He just listens to people and tells them what they think. That's why he has to be one-up on

Clouseau undercover as Toulouse Lautrec.

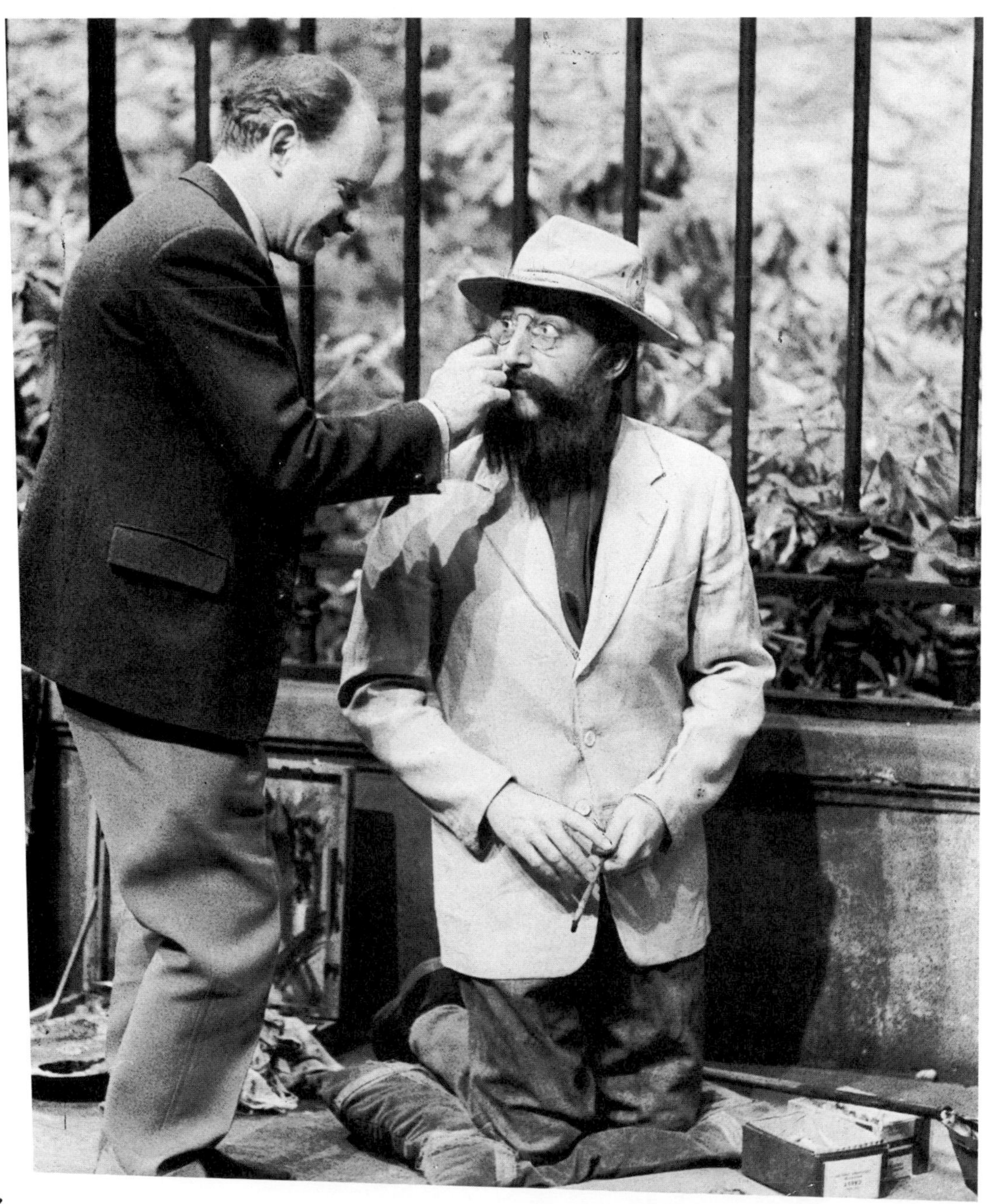

everybody. In the sequel, *A Shot in the Dark*, the butler came in while Clouseau was playing billiards and said, "There's a telephone call for you, Inspector Clouseau," and he says, "Ah, yes, that will be for me," because he wants to be the first to know.

'He is like a Buster Keaton character, fearless, bold and serenely confident that in the end he will triumph. But if I had to define his outstanding trait in one word, it would be purity.

'I gave him a French/English accent. It's not pure French because you have to be very careful with the French accent, apart from Maurice Chevalier's. I wanted to get some other sound.'

Then mid-way through filming the sequel, *A Shot in the Dark, Sellers* was in France where he met a concierge who used words like 'burmp' and 'murth'. It was like manna from heaven and Sellers immediately set about incorporating this curious pronunciation into the film. 'You'll find,' he said, 'if you look at the original Panther, that the sound changed for *A Shot in the Dark* and Clouseau started to say a word like bump in a pursed way, similar to speech patterns based on the actual French language. After that, I started searching through the scripts to find some words I could play with – like "officer of the leu (law)" – which would set people off.'

Clouseau's strangulated vowels quickly reduced everyone on set to helpless wrecks. For Blake Edwards, it became something of a nightmare trying to complete a scene before the cast broke up laughing. On *A Shot in the Dark*, he was particularly keen to get the penultimate scene in the movie shot before the weekend break. It was the scene in the drawing-room where Clouseau, endeavouring to unmask the villain, talked to George Sanders about Elke Sommer setting a 'burmp' on her head. Clouseau went on to describe the 'murths' flying out of the cupboard. Sanders said they were 'moths' and Clouseau agreed. That was what he had just said – 'murths'. At that point, Sellers and Sanders started giggling and every time they tried it after that, the corpsing got worse. By now it was the middle of the Friday afternoon and Edwards was getting nowhere fast. So he pulled out a wad of bank notes and announced: 'The next guy who laughs doubles that, and it's beer money for the crew.' On the next take, Sellers went straight away. Edwards said: 'That's going to cost you £80' and Sellers' chauffeur Bert Mortimer duly placed the money on the pile. But the threat of fines proved no deterrent. Sellers was just about to begin yet another take when, sobbing uncontrollably with laughter, he spluttered to Edwards: 'Right, I'll double the money again but you'll have to do it Monday.' What had set him off that time was catching a glimpse of George Sanders studying his face in a mirror, rehearsing how not to laugh, for fear of being £160 out of pocket! Wisely, Edwards agreed to do the scene on Monday after all.

In between the first two *Pink Panther* films, Sellers starred in the movie which, along with *I'm All Right, Jack*, he would later hail as his favourite role – Stanley

Kubrick's controversial black comedy *Dr. Strangelove, or How I Learned to Stop Worrying and Love the Bomb.* 'I'd do anything Kubrick wanted to make,' enthused Sellers, 'film the phone book, anything. I think he and John Boulting are two directors who've really got into me and I feel I've produced near to my ultimate best as an actor with them.' Notorious for being dissatisfied with his work, Sellers paid *Dr. Strangelove* the rare accolade of describing it as 'a wonderful film'.

Sellers played three roles in the film – US President Merkin Muffley, RAF Captain Lionel Mandrake and the title character, a mad Nazi-American inventor with an artificial arm. Kubrick's idea was to achieve a 'satiric symmetry' in which 'everywhere you turn there is some version of Peter Sellers holding the fate of the world in his hands.' To this end, he also wanted Sellers to play two other

Dr. Strangelove. . .

parts – Major 'King' Kong and General Buck Turgidson. But when Sellers broke an ankle, Slim Pickens took over the role of Kong. As for Turgidson, Sellers didn't like the role and thought it was too physically demanding to take on so much. The part went to George C. Scott.

Sellers revealed how he based Dr.

. . . bore a resemblance to Captain Mandrake.

Strangelove's voice on one of the crew. 'On the set, we had a special stills guy called Weegee, who is now dead. He was very famous, and he took a lot of pictures for *Life* magazine in the old days. When

Sellers and George C. Scott in *Dr Strangelove.*

all the hoods used to get riddled with bullets, he was always the first photographer there, and he'd get as good a shot as possible for the Mafia, and he got $25 from *Life*. He used to talk in a strange little voice like, "Hey, Peter, I really have an idea for a shot here." So I put a German accent on top of Weegee's.'

After finishing *Dr. Strangelove*, Sellers made one more film before *A Shot in the Dark*, venturing back to America for *The World of Henry Orient*, the story of a charismatic concert pianist, somewhere in the void between Liberace and Mrs Mills. While filming in New York, Sellers invited a young female fan out to meet him. At the airport he hid out of sight while his secretary Hattie Stevenson and chauffeur Bert Mortimer greeted the girl. To Sellers' horror, she was obese and, after booking her into a room at the Plaza Hotel (where he too was staying), he informed her over the phone that he would meet her when she had lost weight. After three weeks' intensive dieting, the girl had shed 30lb. whereupon Sellers actually proposed to her and presented her with an expensive engagement ring. But apparently he then became bored with the whole thing and the girl was sent on her way. Even by Sellers' standards, it was a bizarre incident.

Sellers casting *The World of Henry Orient*.

Roy Boulting

Roy and his twin brother John were leading figures in the post-war film industry. In the Forties they were responsible for such gritty dramas as Thunder Rock and Brighton Rock, and in the fifties they concentrated on mildly anarchic comedies such as There's a Girl in My Soup and I'm All Right, Jack.

In 1958 John Redway, a great friend who also represented my brother John and me, said to us, 'Do you ever listen to *The Goon Show*?' We hadn't. He said, 'There's a chap on it called Sellers and I think he's a brilliant comedian.'

John and I listened to the Goons and we saw what Redway meant, so we arranged to meet Peter. I was just about to start shooting a film called *Carlton-Browne of the F.O.* and I thought, let's have a go with him, and in the meantime let's write in for him the part of chief shop-steward in *I'm All Right, Jack,* which we had also recently acquired, and John started work on the script with John Harvey.

Peter didn't, at first, want to do *I'm All Right, Jack;* he couldn't see that it was funny. John and I talked and decided Peter should do a test. Because he was so good, but didn't really know why he was so good, we wanted him to see himself on the screen playing a character role of this kind. Peter agreed. The costume and the little moustache helped him along the road but what clinched it was when one works committee, who happened to have entered at the start of the scene, started to laugh and then they all roared with laughter. Once Peter saw the test, he had no more doubts. He loved Kite and his performance was astonishingly good - it was outstanding.

Peter was a natural. All that he had to learn from John and myself was that you don't have to 'act' if you're thinking right; you don't have to project if you're thinking the part and therefore living the part, because it's going to come out on screen.

I remember one day when we were finishing at twelve, I told Peter to go off and relax as I wouldn't be wanting him until three o'clock for the next scene. He went off and when he returned to the set he came up to me and said 'Roy, I want you to see this, I've bought a new car!' He'd bought it between twelve and three and what's more, on the following day he sold it!

No matter what is said which may appear to be detrimental to Sellers, the fact is that all over the world there are millions of people who take great pleasure from the work he did. I can think of no other comedian actor who has created such a variety of characters. His ability to produce characters of such diversity and with such assurance makes him the greatest talent this country has produced since Charlie Chaplin.

Burt Kwouk

Burt Kwouk played the part of Cato in the Pink Panther films.

Those fights between Cato and Clouseau have become one of the great running gags in motion-picture history, but none of us really knew what we were doing, and I think it shows. You had these two guys who think they are the greatest Martial Arts exponents of all time, and all they succeed in doing is smashing up the set. Although Peter and I kind of knew about Martial Arts, any expert looking at those fights will spot that everything's a little bit wrong. We just did what came naturally to us, which wasn't always quite right. But no one ever got hurt.

We'd turn up, stand around on the set and then wonder what to do: it's very difficult to script a fight. You physically have to get there and say, 'What have we got? What's the space? What's the furniture? What can we do?' You have a general plan - you know how the fight's going to end every time because the phone rings - and you make it up as you go along. After knocking each other about we'd just stand up and get on with the next bit. There were a lot of unscripted moments and Blake didn't attempt to tell us what to do. He'd just say to us, 'Go away and come back with something.'

Peter was the last of the great film actors like Guinness. His roles were greatly contrasted - they were different people, like different actors. Being a movie star is different from being an actor, and Peter was both.

Working with him over lots of pictures and knowing him so long, I started to realise how complicated he was. Since he died people have dwelt on the dark side of Peter Sellers. Of course he had a dark side, we all do, but that's not the side of him that I saw. He never gave me a hard time; I never had any difficulties with him. We liked each other very much and got on very well. I want him to be remembered with fun.

Sellers marries Britt Ekland

Chapter 5

Clouseau Makes A Comeback

'I'm not deaded, I tell you. I'm alive. Thinks... "I hope so".'
Peter Sellers in Bluebottle mode sending a message to the world from his hospital bed following his heart attacks in April 1964.

While filming *A Shot in the Dark*, Sellers had met Britt Ekland, a glamorous Swedish actress seventeen years his junior. Within ten days, he had proposed and the couple were married on 19 February 1964. Sellers knew his instincts were correct because Maurice Woodruff had predicted that he would marry a woman with the initials B.E. But after just 46 days of marriage, their world was shattered when Sellers suffered a series of eight heart attacks during which he was clinically dead for two and a half minutes.

He said later: 'I just thought I kept dozing off. Then I'd hear that klaxon go off and I'd wake up to see four or five guys standing around my bed. So I'd say, "Hey, what are you cats doing here?" I didn't know it, but I wasn't dozing off – I was dying. You'd feel OK, chatting with these chaps, then you'd suddenly feel "Ah – here we go again".'

Advised to rest for at least a year, Sellers outlined his immediate plans to *Life* magazine, stating that he had ordered 'a nice, fast, new car – my 84th, a blue Ferrari' and was planning 'to try out all these silly new steps I've been seeing on TV, like the Watusi. I've even invented my own new dance. I call mine

Sellers on the set of *Kiss Me Stupid*, before ill-health forced him to quit

Rehearsing a scene in *Kiss Me Stupid.*

The Gas Stove.'

His illness forced him to drop out of Billy Wilder's *Kiss Me, Stupid* and for Sellers' next film, *What's New, Pussycat?* (the screenplay for which was written by a young comedian named Woody Allen), producer Charles K. Feldman was obliged to pay $360,000 out of his own pocket to insure against his star dying in the course of filming. Donning a black pageboy wig and black velvet suit to play neurotic German psychiatrist Dr Fritz Fassbender, Sellers demonstrated that his brush with death had in no way diminished his genius although Allen was said to be less than pleased about widespread changes to his script, many of which were jotted down on the back of contraceptive packets by Sellers and co-star Peter O'Toole.

Alas, Sellers' brilliance was to be in short supply over the next few years as his career and personal life plunged into the doldrums. He had scarcely endeared himself to American movie moguls with

Sellers and Ursula Andress in the star-studded *Casino Royale.*

comments he had made about Hollywood following his brief stint on *Kiss Me, Stupid* and now he found himself at the centre of another unhappy film, *Casino Royale*, in which David Niven played

Secret Agent Evelyn Tremble.

007s Vesper Lynd and Evelyn Tremble.

James Bond. Sellers was at his most insecure, refusing to work with co-star Orson Welles and becoming involved in a fist-fight with his old friend Joe McGrath. Typically, after having McGrath sacked as director on *Casino Royale*, Sellers picked him again three years later to direct *The Magic Christian.*

The death of his mother Peg at the age of 72 on 30 January 1967 deepened Sellers' depression. A succession of film flops – two with his wife – hastened the deterioration of their marriage and left him increasingly vulnerable and unpredictable. For his part, he was convinced that the heart attacks had damaged his brain in some way and that this contributed greatly to his irritability.

The pressures of fame became ever more onerous, particularly as the public expected him to be funny at all times. Sellers recalled: 'I remember when I was filming in Paris, a woman came up to me and said, "I hear you're foonayer than Ustinov." I said, "Madam, I couldn't be foonay if you paid me a million pounds." "Well I'm certainly not doing that," she said and walked off.

'The thing that people never realise is that for me to walk into a room, any room, is sheer torture. They expect me to make them laugh – to put on a funny voice, to do an imitation. That's what

Sellers in *The Magic Christian*

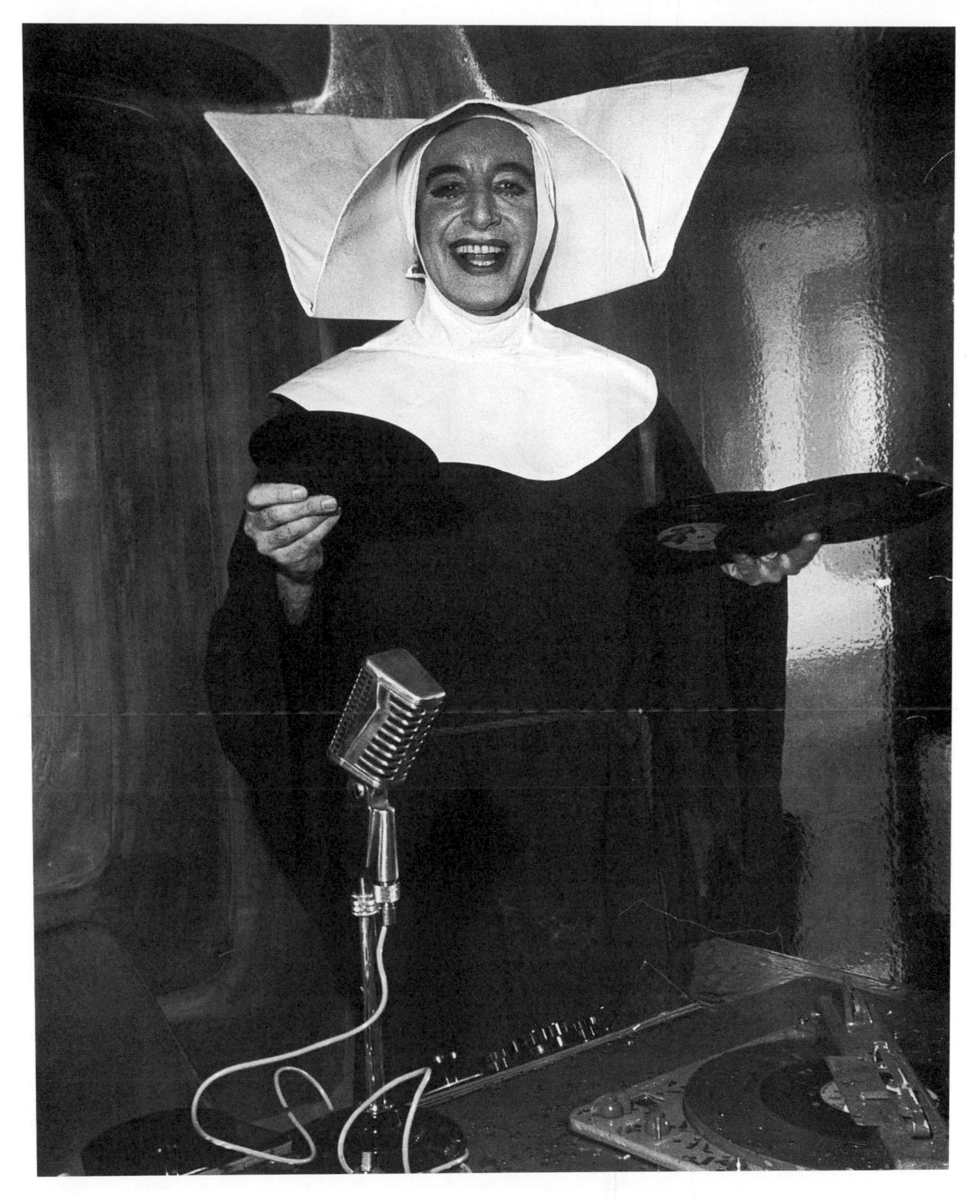

With Ringo Star filming *The Magic Christian.*

Sellers' 15-year-old son Michael (above left) makes his first screen appearance in *The Magic Christian*.

success and fame of a kind do for you, and it isn't easy to live with. I am not essentially a funny man. To me, I am a complete stranger – I haven't a clue who Peter Sellers is. I have no personality of my own, you see – I have no concrete image of myself. That is why I always put on so much make-up – a disguise. Even if I didn't need these glasses, I'd still wear them. When I look in the mirror, what I see is someone who has never grown up –

a crashing sentimentalist who alternates between great heights and black depths.

'There is nothing about me as a person that I could put on the screen. To see me in the cinema would be one of the dullest experiences that anyone could imagine. I'm a character actor, not a star, and when I finish a picture I feel a horrible sudden loss of identity.'

Sellers was only happy when he could hide within a character. 'When I assume a character it takes over my personality completely. I find myself slipping into an almost trancelike state. The character takes me over – he exists in my body. I don't have to ask myself how he would react to this or that. I know the character acts for me. During the production of a movie, I lunch alone in my dressing-room to keep the trance intact. I try not to talk to anyone, or become interested in anything that would not interest the character.'

He hated being recognised as himself and quickly developed a knack for discouraging unwanted attention. 'The other day a man in a restaurant thrust his face into mine saying, "You are Peter Sellers, aren't you?" I replied, "Not today" and went on my way.'

Sellers had always been superstitious

'I have no concrete image of myself. That is why I always put on so much make-up – a disguise' – Sellers.

and had a particular bee in his bonnet about empty matchboxes. In his early days, he once signed up for a variety tour without an empty matchbox clutched in his left hand and it flopped. Thereafter, on his way to clinch big deals, he had been known to stop the car and peer into dustbins for empty matchboxes. But in later years his various superstitions – notably his refusal to look at the colours green or purple (the latter, he had been told, was the colour of death) – created headaches for those around him. His assistants had to ensure that no callers were wearing those colours. A casino scene in *The Prisoner of Zenda* had to be re-shot with a red baize instead of green,

Sellers on the set of *Hoffman* (right) and in more relaxed mode off it (below).

while Sellers would not venture on to the set of *Hoffman* to film a restaurant scene until the purple tablecloths had been replaced. He also refused to meet Blake Edwards' mother-in-law because she was wearing a purple coat.

Between the periods of gloom, there were many brighter moments with Sellers the practical joker rarely far beneath the surface. When Goon devotee Prince Charles accepted a lunch invitation from Sellers and Britt Ekland at their Surrey home, he was confronted with ever decreasing portions. With each course, the amount of food set before HRH grew smaller so that by the time cheese and biscuits were served, he was presented with little more than a few crumbs!

Graham Stark once played a splendid prank on Sellers, sending him a letter advertising a battery-operated, life-sized horizontal doll with full moving parts. The doll, which came in kit form, clearly appealed to Sellers who told Stark excitedly: 'Just think what we can do with it . . . especially when we get the motor going!' It was only when Stark was unable to contain his glee any longer that Sellers realised he had been duped. Stark said: 'He joined in the fun but his laugh didn't cover the disappointment.'

Sellers endeavoured to gain his revenge on his friend by teaming up with Blake Edwards to print some fake leaflets promoting a range of newly discovered German virility pills. Apparently Stark swallowed the bait but presumably not the pills.

A similar Sellers joke involved a product known as the Mongolian Monk Penis Enlarging Ointment, the properties of which were self-explanatory. The ointment, which had the added bonus that no Mongolian monk was needed to apply it, was advertised via a series of specially printed leaflets. Sellers revealed that customers could hardly wait to send off their postal orders to the stipulated address in Copenhagen – from where an accomplice mailed back tubs of rancid garlic butter.

Goldie Hawn and Sellers at Shepperton during the filming of There's a Girl in my Soup.

Another example of Sellers' bizarre sense of humour was his habit of tipping airline pilots in the way one would a taxi driver. After a long transatlantic flight, he would wander up to the cockpit, slip a fiver into the pilot's top jacket pocket and say: 'Nice flight – have a drink on me.' It rarely failed to leave the pilot utterly puzzled.

In 1969, Sellers was divorced from Britt Ekland. In the same year, a BBC documentary *Will the Real Peter Sellers...?* depicted him as a sad, lonely figure. His third marriage, to Miranda Quarry in 1970, was accompanied by a mini-revival in his film career when he was reunited with the Boulting Brothers for *There's a Girl in My Soup.* Sellers played the suave Robert Danvers, basing the character on the Queen's cousin, photographer Patrick Lichfield.

In 1972, as part of the BBC's 50th anniversary celebrations, Sellers joined Milligan, Secombe, Max Geldray and Ray Ellington for *The Last Goon Show Of All.* Before the recording, a telegram was read out from a sailor serving abroad. It said how disappointed he was not to be at the show 'especially as my father and sister are both able to attend. My hair has turned green with envy and my knees have fallen off.' It was signed Charles. The telegram was from Prince Charles, otherwise detained on a destroyer in the Mediterranean. Although Sellers struggled at first to get the right pitch for Bluebottle, the show was a great success due in no small part to Princess Anne having pre-recorded the sound of horses' hooves in the traditional manner of banging two coconut shells together in front of the microphone.

Amidst this series of undistinguished films, *The Optimists of Nine Elms* proved a poignant movie for Sellers. He played Sam, an old-time music hall busker, and the role brought back memories of his own father. During breaks in shooting,

The Goons won an award when *The Last Goon Show of All* sold £75,000 worth of records and tapes.

EXPOSES ALL THE
FACTS AND FIGURES
Seagram's
Directory Enquiries

Sellers, unrecognisable in costume and with a splendid set of false teeth, delighted in entertaining passers-by with an impromptu musical act. At Battersea market, he was overjoyed when a passer-by went up to him and asked: 'Where can I find Peter Sellers?' In Leicester Square, he was told by an irate busker: 'Shove over, mate. You're on my pitch.' Another scene was filmed outside Fulham football ground on matchday with none of the spectators realising that the scruffy old man wandering among them was an international movie star.

By 1975, Sellers' career was at an all-time low. He was once again between wives (having split with Miranda Quarry the previous year) and was reduced to accepting roles with names like Dick Scratcher in the unreleased *Ghost in the Noonday Sun.* Blake Edwards was also going through something of a lean period and thought about restoring his fortunes by reviving the *Pink Panther* series. The idea interested Sir Lew Grade who wanted to produce *The Return of the Pink Panther* as a 26-part TV series before Edwards persuaded him to make it as a film. Sellers had turned down the unsuccessful 1968

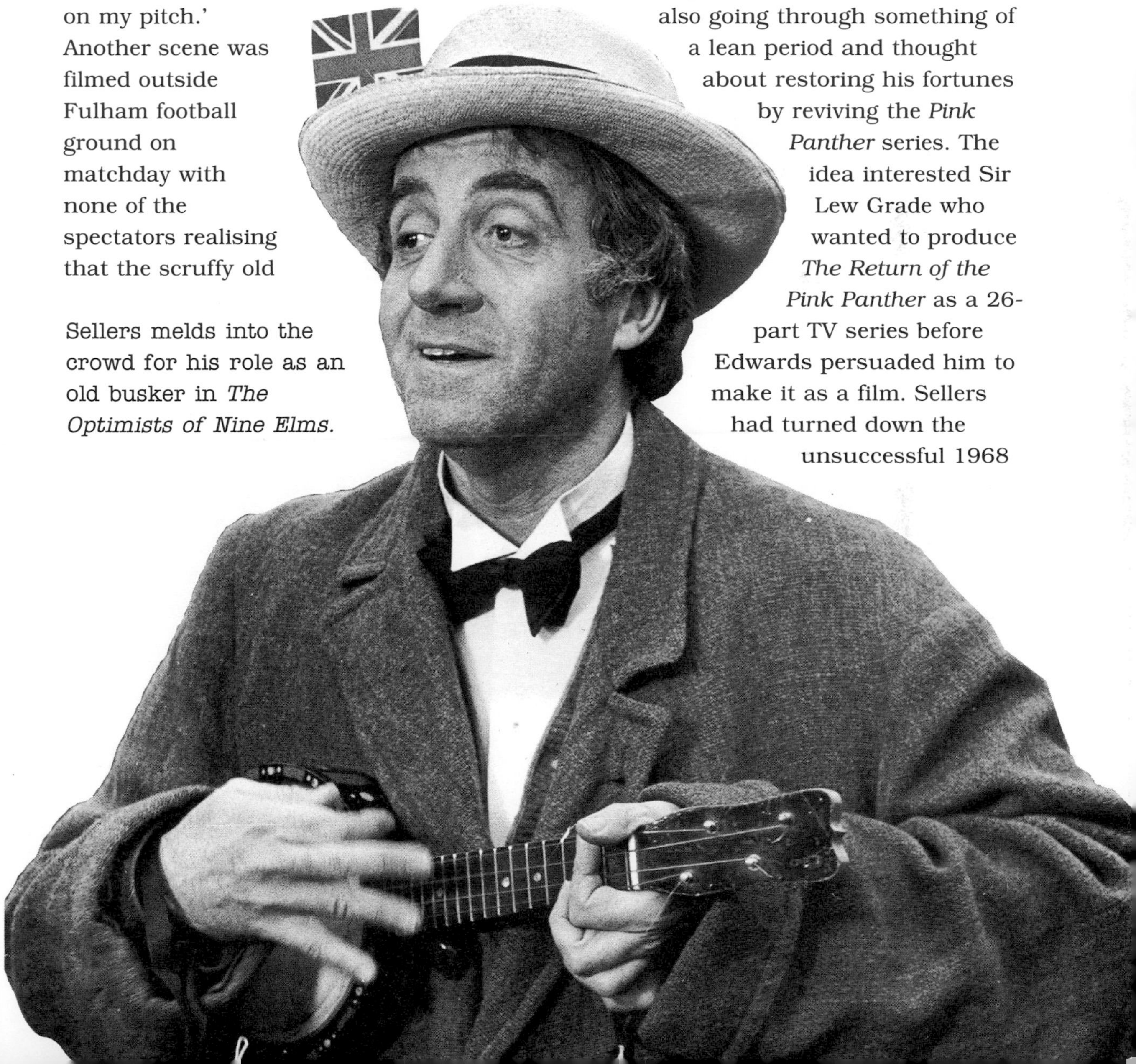

Sellers melds into the crowd for his role as an old busker in *The Optimists of Nine Elms.*

Between shots on *The Return of the Pink Panther*, with co-star Catherine Schell.

film *Inspector Clouseau* (in which the hapless detective was eventually played by Alan Arkin) but now the timing and script appealed to him. It was one of his wiser judgements. *The Return of the Pink Panther* became a massive worldwide hit and re-established Sellers as a major box office attraction.

'Clouseau never died,' revealed Edwards. 'Over the years, Peter and I kept him alive. Peter would call me up with Clouseau's voice on the phone and we'd spend hours thinking up ideas and laughing like crazy.'

Sellers was thrilled at the opportunity

Ready for Cato.

Clouseau, still at the cutting edge of undercover police work in *The Return of the Pink Panther.*

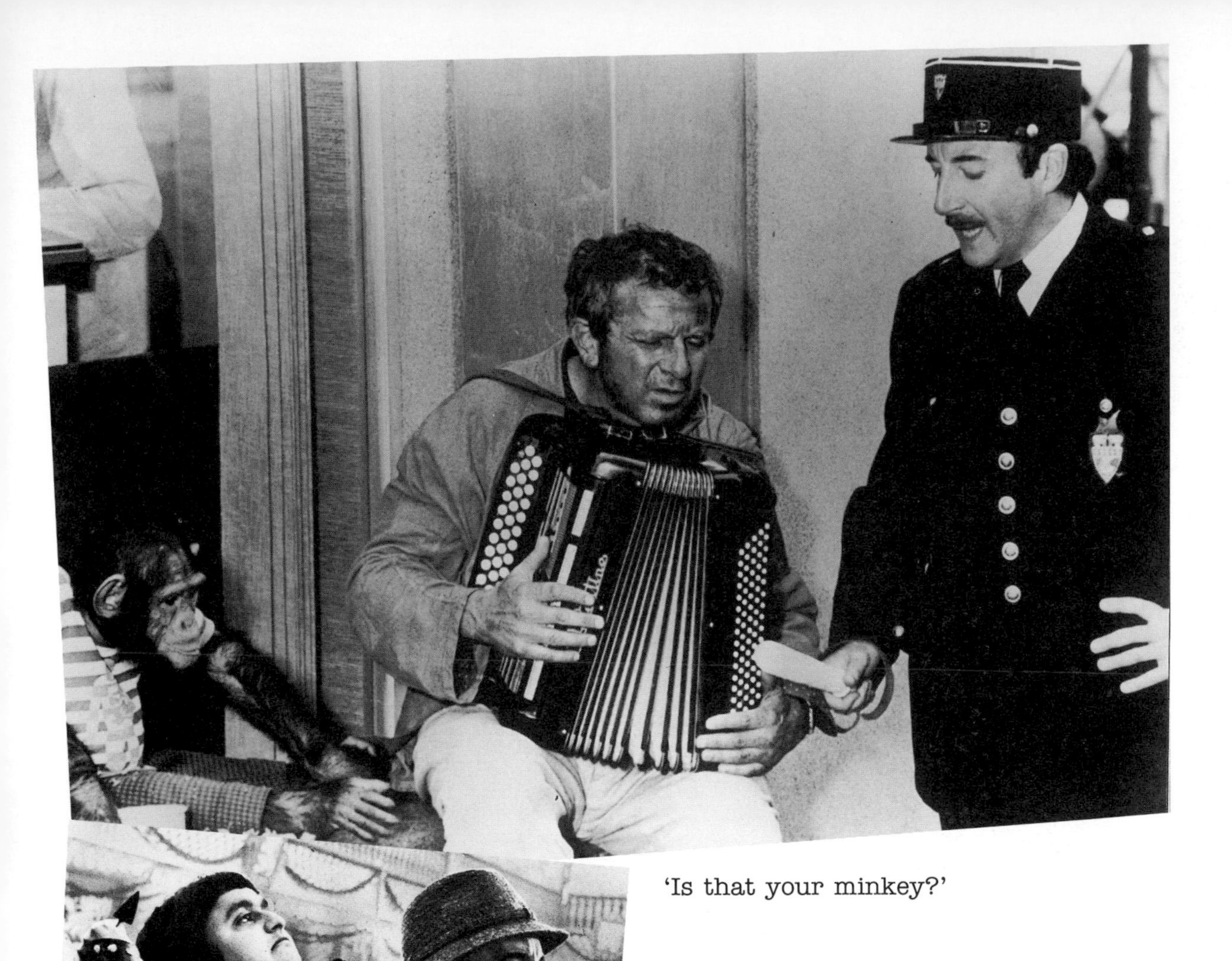

'Is that your minkey?'

to put on the hat and belted raincoat once again. 'When they tried to make the American version of Clouseau, it didn't work,' he said. 'Blake's the only one who can direct it, and I'm the only one who can play him. I know Clouseau so well he's almost a part of me. In fact, there's a bit of Clouseau in all of us. We all know that the terrible and embarrassing things that happen to him could easily happen to any one of us. Blake and I are like Laurel and Hardy together. We work out

A would-be assassin is thwarted in *The Pink Panther Strikes Again.*

Clouseau as Norwegian fisherman with wooden leg and Clouseau as dentist strongly reminiscent of Einstein.

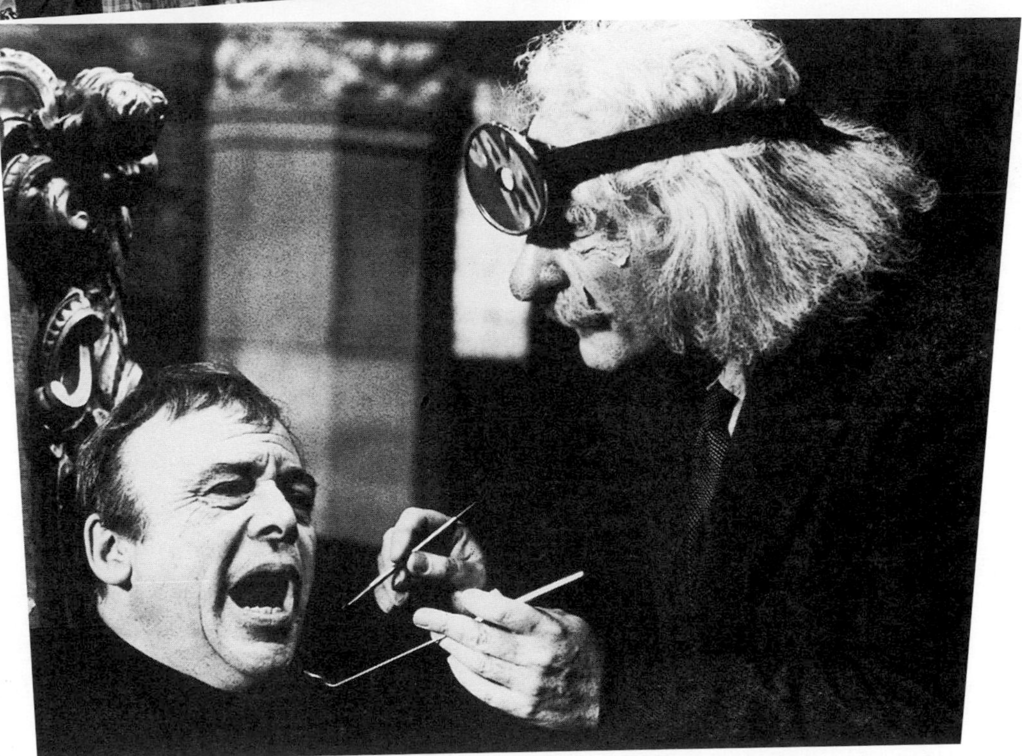

Close-up with Valerie Leon in *Revenge of the Pink Panther.*

Chief Inspector Dreyfus is pushed to the limit.

each gag to the tiniest detail, and still ad-lib a lot of it when the cameras start turning.'

Prince Charles was a huge admirer of *The Return of the Pink Panther*. In one of his frequent letters to Sellers (whom he often addressed as 'Dear Bluebottle), the Prince wrote of seeing the film in

Clouseau grows a beard and becomes an abbot in *Revenge of the Pink Panther*

Montreal and crying with laughter so much that he wet the dress of the woman sitting next to him.

Clouseau's accent ran riot with Sellers at his most inventive, playing endless games with the French language. He said at the time: 'When they are asking about cash in English, the French say: "Have you any *mo*ney?" If you put a "k" in there, it becomes monkey, so I thought it was wild when Clouseau said monkey."' By the time it reached the screen where the demoted Clouseau was giving grief to a blind beggar, 'monkey' had become 'minkey' and the land was rife with filmgoers conversing in Clouseau-speak. In the summer of 1975, how many hoteliers must have despaired at yet another guest asking for a 'rim'?

Now that Sellers was back as flavour of the month, the offers of scripts poured in. His next movie was Neil Simon's *Murder by Death* in which Sellers, playing Chinese detective Sidney Wang resplendent in a droopy Fu Manchu moustache, was re-united with his old idol Alec Guinness.

Although he had always detested repetition, Sellers was so buoyed by the reaction to Clouseau's reappearance that he agreed to make *The Pink Panther Strikes Again* and *The Revenge of the Pink Panther.* He said of Clouseau: 'It's the only part I've played that, wherever I go, people ask me when I'm going to play it again. An actor, especially a character actor, has to consider public

N.Y.P.D.

demand.' His participation in the films was less strenuous than before. The hilarious martial arts scenes with Cato were done by a stunt double and on *Revenge*, which saw Clouseau – 'I glide through the underworld like a shadow' – disguised in turn as Toulouse-Lautrec, a Hong Kong coolie, a Mafia Godfather, a Swedish herring merchant and a Catholic priest, Sellers wore a pacemaker following another heart scare. He brushed aside the restrictions of the device. 'Once you get used to the fact that you're partly bionic, you forget about it.'

Although the *Panther* films had become the highest-grossing comedy series in movie history, Sellers stated after *Revenge:* 'I've honestly had enough of Clouseau – I've got nothing more to give.'

Instead he chose to star with his fourth wife Lynne Frederick in a remake of *The Prisoner of Zenda.* Sellers was less than impressed by the finished product and at the end of a private screening, he got up, walked to the door, turned and said to

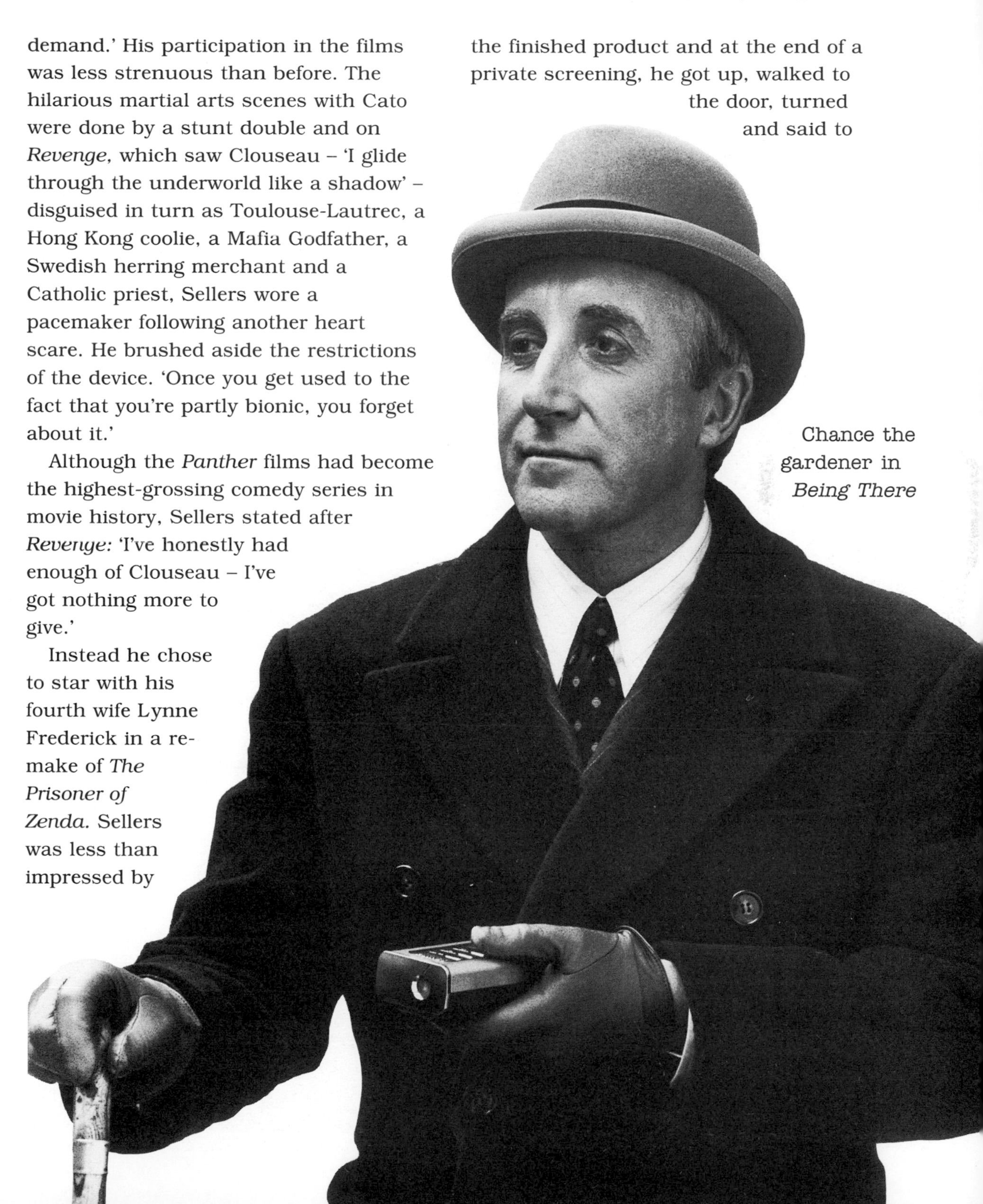

Chance the gardener in *Being There*

Sellers' performance in *Being There* is completely unlike any other in his career, and won him an Oscar nomination.

producer Walter Mirisch: 'I have only one comment to make – my lawyers will be in touch with you.' His timing, as ever, was impeccable.

For eight years, Sellers had been eager to do a film of Jerzy Kosinski's 1971 novel *Being There.* The part which Sellers coveted was that of the simple-minded gardener Chance and over the years he had besieged Kosinski with cards signed 'Chance'. When Kosinski finally relented, Sellers had problems getting the right voice for Chance before inspiration arrived in the unlikely form of Stan Laurel. Sellers had always been a big fan of Laurel and often travelled with a large autographed photo of the comedian. Analysing the part, he decided to base Chance's voice on that of Laurel, adding an American twist for good measure. Sellers' performance earned him rave reviews and a second Oscar nomination for Best Actor (he had previously been short-listed for *Dr. Strangelove*), but he lost out to Dustin Hoffman for *Kramer vs. Kramer.*

Just as he had always consulted Maurice Woodruff about his career, Sellers now claimed to have frequent discussions with his mother about which role to take. This proved a shade disconcerting to some Hollywood executives, including *Being There* producer Andrew Braunsberg. Prior to shooting, Sellers told Braunsberg: 'I'm not

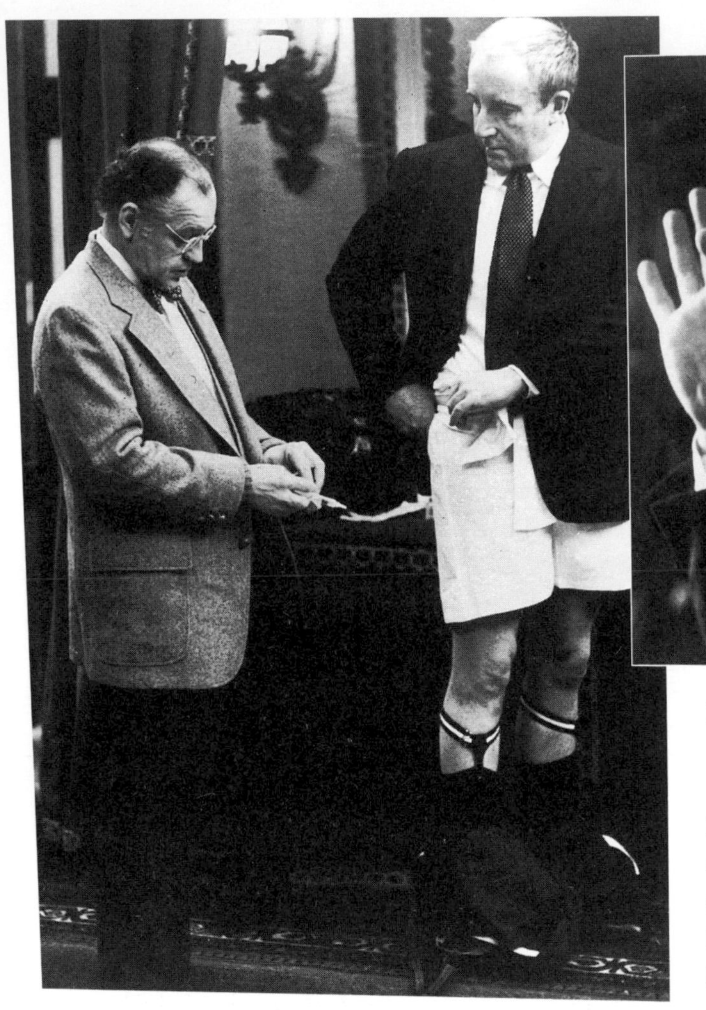

More scenes from *Being There*.

getting enough cut in this film. I spoke to my mother and she told me that I've got to come and ask for more.' Braunsberg relayed the news to the Lorimar office: 'He's sticking out for more money, he's spoken to his mother.' The guy in the office was keen to negotiate. 'Well give me her phone number,' he said. 'I'll talk to her.' To which Braunsberg replied: 'She's been dead for ten years...'

Sellers' conversations with his late mother often possessed a Goon-like quality, none more so than when he and Miranda Quarry were living in Ireland and Sellers tried to use the powers of spiritualism to get in touch with a lost hen. 'Miranda decided when we were in Ireland that she'd like to have some chickens. So we bought a broody hen and some day-old chicks. Well, the hen got lost and we thought a fox must have got it, and Miranda was in a bit of a state.

'When it had been gone for three days we decided to have a seance and when Peg came through, I said: "Darling, do you know where the hen has gone?"

'"Of course I know," she said. "It's up in the rafters."

'"What rafters?" I said.

'"In the stable outside," she said.

'"Can you hang on for a minute?" I said. "We'll take a look." And we went out

With his wife Lynn Frederick on the set of his last film *The Fiendish Plot of Dr Fu Manchu*

and looked around, but it was pitch dark in the stable and we couldn't see anything. "It's not there," I said.

'"Of course it's there," she said. "Go and have another look. But don't be too long. I'm not sodding about all night looking for a hen."

'Well we still couldn't find it. But the next day Bert (Mortimer) went out and there in a dark corner was the hen.'

In the autumn of 1979, Sellers began work on what was to be his final film, *The Fiendish Plot of Dr. Fu Manchu,* in which he played both the evil Fu and his Scotland Yard adversary, Nayland Smith. 'The poor blighter is 168 years old,' Sellers said of Fu. 'His henchmen have to plug him into a wall socket every morning to keep him ticking. The police of six continents are searching for him. And he still hasn't conquered the civilised world, defiled its women or pillaged its cities. The man deserves some sympathy.'

The scene where Fu disguises himself as a chef was shot in Paris's Parc St. Cloud. In his white chefs hat and Fu's rubber wrinkles, Sellers was once again unrecognisable and used the welcome anonymity to spin some tall tales to curious members of the Paris public. He told one group of passers-by that the banquet of Oriental food was a picnic for a touring ping-pong team. Others were solemnly informed that various varieties of soy sauce were being tested like wines. He even managed to convince one onlooker that he was the owner of a genuine Chinese restaurant and had moved his business into the park while it was being redecorated!

Following *Fu Manchu,* Sellers had decided after all to give one more airing to Clouseau – this time without the involvement of Blake Edwards. Sellers was writing *The Romance of the Pink Panther* with Jim Moloney and was optimistic about the outcome. 'I think we've come up with some good stuff – a different slant on Clouseau. And having him in love should be interesting. If this is to be the last *Pink Panther* film, I'm determined that it's got to be a good one.'

But Sellers' friends and acquaintances were alarmed at how frail he had suddenly become. His weak heart appeared to be taking its toll. Shortly after 2 p.m. on 22 July 1980, he collapsed into an armchair in his suite at London's Dorchester Hotel, having suffered a massive heart attack. He was rushed to the Middlesex Hospital where he died two days later.

Sellers said that he wanted to be remembered above all as a Goon and ironically his fatal heart attack occurred on the day he was due to enjoy a dinner reunion with Milligan and Secombe, the first such get-together for eight years. But there was still more than an element of Goonery at his celebrity-packed funeral on 26 July when he was cremated to the sound of Glenn Miller's 'In the Mood'. Milligan had once asked Sellers: 'Any special hymn you'd like to have played when you go?' 'Yes, "In the Mood",' came the reply. 'Is that in Hymns Ancient and Modern?' inquired Milligan. 'No, it's in Glenn Miller.'

Peter Sellers always liked to have the last laugh.

POLICE

Eric Sykes

Eric Sykes knew Peter Sellers long before the Goon Shows, and has many fond memories of their friendship, but it was through the Goons that they developed a special bond, as Eric explains:

'To help take the pressure off Spike, I wrote some of the *Goon Shows* – all I was really doing was copying Spike's style and using the characters that were already there. I wrote a few with Spike and a few where we did alternate weeks.

'Then, I turned up one Sunday morning with a script for the read-through and there was total silence after they'd finished it. Peter Eton was producing. He said, "Well, we don't think it's very funny, Eric."

'I was so angry because I didn't think they were trying – they weren't putting any guts into it – and I walked out. We always used to go and have dinner after the show at a restaurant in Edgware Road. That night I had dinner there early, by myself, but as I left the restaurant, a taxi drew up and Peter Sellers got out. He was actually crying, and he ran up to me and put his arms around me and he said, "Eric, that was the best show we've ever done."

'I took a great shine to Peter for wanting to come up and tell me that.'

Sellers and Sykes would go on to work together on a number of different shows, including the television *Saturday Spectaculars* which Sykes presented live, but Sellers was frustrated about not being able to participate in one particular project.

'I remember explaining to Peter an idea I had about two men carrying a plank across London,' Sykes recalls, 'and he was in fits of laughter. He said, "I must do it. I must play the other part." I was later given a date from Bernard Delfont to make *The Plank* – a feature film starring Peter sellers and me. Unfortunately, Peter's other commitments meant that he had to pull out of the film, but I was able to bring in Tommy Cooper, who was also a friend of mine.'

Having missed out on the opportunity to make *The Plank* with Sykes, Sellers was determined to make it up to his friend.

'Peter was upset because he thought he'd let me down,' says Sykes, 'so when I was doing the television shows with Hattie Jacques, I asked him if he would play one of the parts [a villain] in it. It was the only television sit-com he'd ever done and he was absolutely brilliant in it. We didn't see anything of Peter after the final rehearsal when everyone went to make up. The next time we saw him was on set, with the cameras rolling when he walked through the front door. We just looked at him and Hat and I were both both gone. He'd had a crew cut and he'd blacked out some of his teeth. I couldn't stop laughing.'

Sellers' temperament and attitude to those around him has come in for a great deal of criticism in the past, but Sykes believes he knew the real Peter Sellers.

'Peter, as he was himself, was a lovely man. He was a very retiring person. It was only when he donned the mantle of the character he was playing that he became something different. Then the character took him over. For instance, when we were making *Educating Archie* one of the cast, a very nice chap, sadly died. Well, Peter and I were having dinner in a restaurant a few weeks after this when suddenly, I heard this fellow's voice, the one who had died! I looked across the table and he was sitting right there! The hair on the back of my neck went up. Then I realised it was only Peter. He burst into laughter. He hadn't done anything special but he had this strange ability to change the way he looked. Peter could do an instant impression of anyone he'd just met. I think that Rory Bremner is a brilliant impressionist, but in all fairness I have to say that Peter would have left him standing.'

One of the reasons that Sellers and Sykes became such firm friends was that they shared a love of bizarre situations and knew that whenever they got together, they would be able to have a few laughs.

'Peter had a tremendous sense of fun,' agrees Sykes. 'When he was in the theatre as a stand-up comic, he was always changing his routine. He didn't like doing the same thing all the time. He had an eight minute spot and one day, instead of doing his act, he went on stage with a chair and a little green beize card table. On it was a wind up gramaphone and he'd brought a record. He said, "Good evening, ladies and gentlemen. I know you're going to like this one." He put on the record, sat down on the chair and played this old 78 of Jack Payne and his band singing *Red Hot Rythym.* At the end of it, of course, the audience applauded. Peter said, "I knew you'd like that and you're going to like the other side even better!"

'He turned it over and that was his eight minutes!'

Despite the fact that Sellers saw great success as a solo performer on stage, Sykes maintains that his real calling lay elsewhere.

'Peter wasn't made to be a stand-up comic, although he had done that and he was good at it. He was made to play different roles and whatever role he was asked to play, he did brilliantly. Think of how funny he was in the *Pink Panther* films as Monsieur Clouseau. He made that part his own. At the same time, he could play something straight as he did in *Being There* when he was nominated for an Oscar. A straight part, but he had the brilliance of timing to be able to pull it off. He certainly deserved an Oscar for that role.'

Even when they weren't able to meet up, Sellers and Sykes managed to keep each other amused.

'He was such a funny letter writer,' says Sykes. 'We used to write these strange, surreal letters to each other. After he'd been in the show with Hat and me [at the end of which Sellers' character went to jail], I wrote to him addressing it "4683784, Cell Block 6" and in the letter I thanked him and said how lovely it was to see him last week and that Hat was sending him a cake but warning him not to bite into it straight away or offer it to anyone because inside there was a power drill. He wrote back saying thanks for the power drill but could you send me some mince pies because I need a plug!

'I wish I'd kept his letters, but I don't suppose he kept mine. The thought was always there, anyway. We always kept each other in our thoughts.'

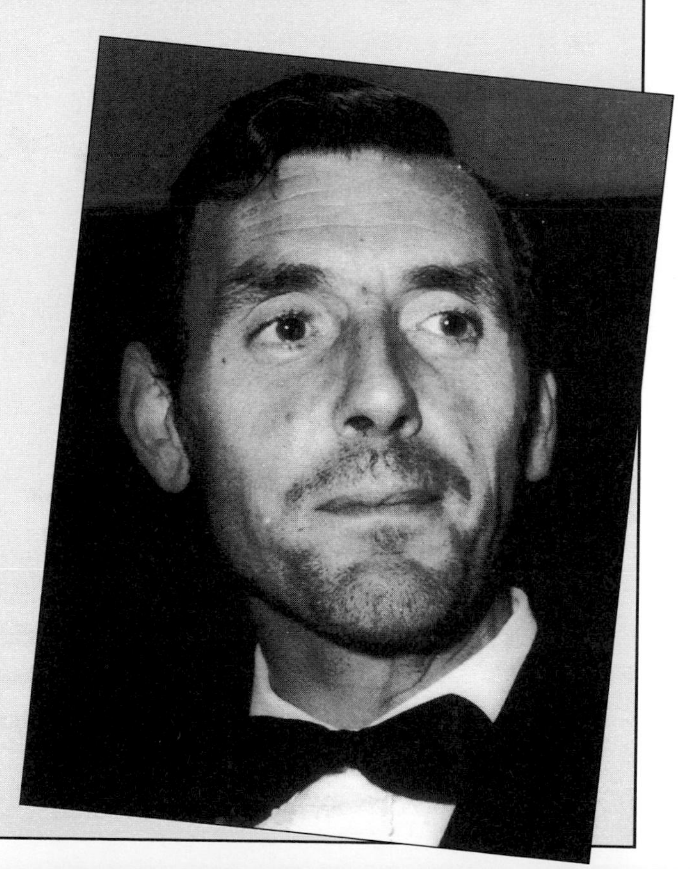

This sinister quintet pose with their unsuspecting landlady Katie Johnson, whose house they are using to plan a banknote robbery in *The Ladykillers*.

The Chronology Bit

or Everything You Ever Wanted To Know About Peter Sellers' Career... But Didn't Know Who To Ask

INTRODUCTION

What follows is a chronological listing of all of the film appearances that Peter Sellers made during the course of his career, but as this book clearly demonstrates, cinema wasn't the only medium that he worked in. His credits span television, radio, theatre, the odd cartoon voice-over or two, commercials and records. So, any attempt to present a definitive catalogue of all of this would probably end up doubling the length of this book!

The notes on films and records are actually comprehensive, but with all of the variety work that he did on stage and his countless guest appearances on radio and television, these latter categories become rather more difficult to complete. Therefore, all of the known credits that the research for this volume has unearthed are included, and any additional information that comes to light after this text sees print will be added to any future revisions of this book...

Film Appearances

Feature Films

Noted In Order of Theatrical Release

Note: For films where Sellers was involved in any capacity other than just acting, any additional credits are noted as seen on screen for the said productions.

1951 **PENNY POINTS TO PARADISE**
Sellers as Major Arnold P'Fringe
With: Harry Secombe, Spike Milligan, Alfred Marks, Bill Kerr and Paddy O'Neil
Screenplay by John Ormonde
Directed by Tony Young
Running Time: 77 minutes
(Black & White)
Released: 12th October 1951

1952 **DOWN AMONG THE Z MEN**
Sellers as Colonel Bloodnok
With: Harry Secombe, Spike Milligan, Michael Bentine, Carole Carr, Graham Stark and Andrew Timothy
Screenplay by Jimmy Grafton and Francis Charles
Directed by Maclean Rogers
Running Time: 82 minutes
(Black & White)
Released: 12th July 1952

1954 **ORDERS ARE ORDERS**
Sellers as Private Goffin
With: Brian Harper, Margot Grahame, Sidney James, Raymond Huntley, Tony Hancock and Bill Fraser
Screenplay by Geoffrey Orme and Donald Taylor
Directed by Donald Platenghi
Running Time: 78 minutes
(Black & White)
Released: 30th September 1954

JOHN AND JULIE
Sellers as Police Constable Diamond
With: Colin Gibson, Leslie Dudley, Moira Lister, Wilfrid Hyde-White, Sidney James and Megs Jenkins
Screenplay by William Fairchild
Directed by William Fairchild
Running Time: 82 minutes (Colour)
Released: 15th July 1955

1956 **THE LADYKILLERS**
Sellers as Harry Robinson
With: Alec Guinness, Katie Johnson, Danny Green, Herbert Lom, Cecil Parker Jack Warner and Frankie Howerd
Screenplay by William Rose
Directed by Alexander Mackendrick
Running Time: 90 minutes (Colour)
Released: 24th February 1956

1957 **THE SMALLEST SHOW ON EARTH**
Sellers as Percy Quill
With: Bill Travers, Virginia McKenna,

Margaret Rutherford, Bernard Miles and Sidney James
Screenplay by William Rose and John Eldridge
Directed by Basil Dearden
Running Time: 81 minutes
(Black & White)
Released: 11th April 1957

Quill, the projectionist, discusses plans to re-open the Bijou Kinema in *The Smallest Show on Earth*.

1958 THE NAKED TRUTH

Sellers as Sonny MacGregor

With: Terry-Thomas, Dennis Price, Peggy Mount, Shirley Eaton, Georgina Cookson and Kenneth Griffiths
Screenplay by Michael Pertwee
Directed by Mario Zampi
Running Time: 92 minutes
(Black & White)
Released: 2nd January 1958

Michael Dennis (Dennis Price) threatens to reveal details of Sonny MacGregor's private life in his scandalous magazine *The Naked Truth*.

1958 UP THE CREEK

Sellers as Bosun Dockerty

With: David Tomlinson, Wilfrid Hyde-White, Vera Day, Reginald Beckwith and Lionel Jeffries
Screenplay by Val Guest
Directed by Val Guest
Running Time: 83 minutes
(Black & White)
Released: 7th November 1958

Bosun Dockerty stands to attention in *Up The Creek.*

With Terry-Thomas in *tom thumb.*

1958 tom thumb

Sellers as Tony

With: Russ Tamblyn, Bernard Miles, Jessie Matthews, Terry-Thomas, Alan Young, June Thorburn and Ian Wallace
Screenplay by Ladislas Fodor
Directed by George Pal
Running Time: 98 minutes (Colour)
Released: 24th December 1958

1959 THE MOUSE THAT ROARED

Sellers as Count Mountjoy, Tully Bascombe and Duchess Gloriana

With: Jean Seberg, David Kossoff, Leo McKern and William Hartnell
Screenplay by Roger McDougall and Stanley Mann
Based on the novel by Leonard Wibberley
Directed by Jack Arnold
Running Time: 85 minutes (Colour)
Released: 17th July 1959

Crafty, double-dealing Prime Minister Amphibulos of Gallardia is a politician with an eye for the main chance – money – in *Carlton-Browne of the F.O.*

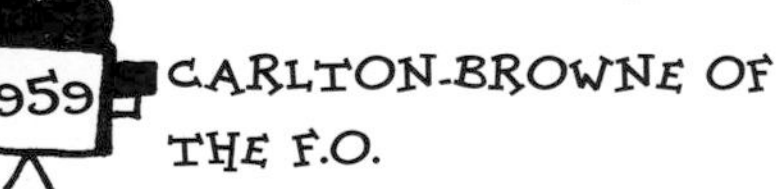

1959 CARLTON-BROWNE OF THE F.O.

Sellers as Amphibulos

With: Terry-Thomas, Ian Bannen, Thorley Walters, Raymond Huntley, John Le Mesurier and Miles Malleson
Screenplay by Roy Boulting and Jeffrey Dell
Directed by Roy Boulting and Jeffrey Dell
(Produced by John Boulting)
Running Time: 88 minutes (Black & White)
Released: 13th March 1959

Peace-loving Tully Bascombe leads the Duchy of Grand Fenwick's gallant force of twenty men to war against America in *The Mouse That Roared.*

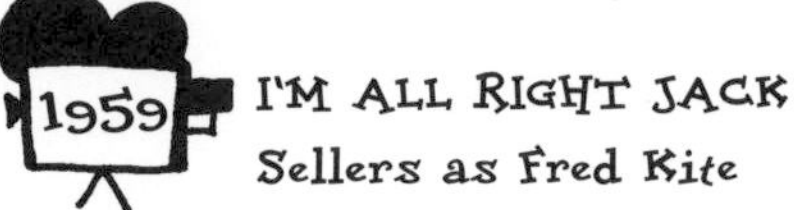

1959 I'M ALL RIGHT JACK

Sellers as Fred Kite

With: Ian Carmichael, Terry-Thomas, Dennis Price, Richard Attenborough, Liz Fraser, Irene Handl, Margaret Rutherford and John Le Mesurier
Screenplay by Frank Harvey, John Boulting and Alan Hackney
Based on the novel by Alan Hackney - 'Private Life'
Directed by John Boulting
(Produced by Roy Boulting)
Running Time: 104 mintues (Black & White)
Released: 13th August 1959

Kite finds domestic work considerably more difficult than his own when his wife goes on strike in *I'm All Right Jack*.

1960 TWO-WAY STRETCH

Sellers as Dodger Lane

With: Bernard Cribbins, Lionel Jeffries, David Lodge, Wilfrid Hyde-White, Irene Handl, Liz Fraser and Maurice Denham
Screenplay by John Warren and Len Heath
Directed by Robert Day
Running Time: 87 minutes (Black & White)
Released: 11th February 1960

1960 THE BATTLE OF THE SEXES

Sellers as Mr Martin

With: Constance Cummings, Robert Morely, Jameson Clark, Donald Pleasence and Ernest Thesiger

Three unrepentant inmates of Huntleigh Prison in *Two-Way Stretch*.

Screenplay by Monja Danischewsky
Based on the novel by James Thurber - *The Catbird Seat*
Directed by Charles Crichton
Running Time: 83 minutes
(Black & White)
Released: 25th February 1960

Mr Martin in *The Battle of the Sexes*.

1960 NEVER LET GO
Sellers as Lionel Meadows
With: Richard Todd, Elizabeth Sellars, Adam Faith, Carol White, Mervyn Johns and David Lodge
Screenplay by Alan Falconer
Directed by John Guillermin
Running Time: 91 minutes
(Black & White)
Released: 2nd June 1960

Lionel Meadows guards his garage in *Never Let Go.*

Dr Ahmed el Kabir examines a patient (Sophia Loren) in *The Millionairess.*

1960 **THE MILLIONAIRESS**
Sellers as Doctor Ahmed el Kabir

With: Sophia Loren, Alistair Sim, Vittorio de Sica, Dennis Price, Alfie Bass and Noel Purcell
Screenplay by Wolf Mankowitz
Based on the play by George Bernard Shaw
Directed by Anthony Asquith
Running Time: 90 minutes (Colour)
Released: 8th October 1960

1961 **MISTER TOPAZE**
Sellers as Albert Topaze

With: Herbert Lom, Leo McKern, Nadia Gray, Martita Hunt, John Neville, Billie Whitelaw, John Le Mesurier and Michael Sellers
Screenplay by Pierre Rouve
Based on the play by Marcel Pagnol - *Topaze*
Directed by Peter Sellers
Running Time: 84 minutes (Colour)
Released: 21st March 1961

1962 **ONLY TWO CAN PLAY**
Sellers as John Lewis

With: Mai Zetterling, Virginia Maskell, Richard Attenborough, Raymond Huntley, Kenneth Griffiths, John Le Mesurier and Graham Stark
Screenplay by Bryan Forbes
Based on the novel by Kingsley Amis - *That Uncertain Feeling*
Directed by Sidney Gillat
Running Time: 106 minutes
(Black & White)
Released: 11th January 1962

Sellers as Mr Topaz in a scene with Herbert Lom and Nadia Gray.

1962 **WALTZ OF THE TOREADORS**
Sellers as General Leo Fitzjohn
With: Margaret Leighton, Dany Robin, Cyril Cusack, John Fraser and Prunella Scales
Screenplay by Wolf Mankowitz
Based on the play by Jean Anouilh
Directed by John Guillermin
Running Time: 105 minutes (Colour)
Released: 12th April 1962

1962 **LOLITA (1962)**
Sellers as Clare Quilty
With: James Mason, Shelley Winters and Sue Lyon
Screenplay by Vladmir Nabokov, based on his novel
Directed by Stanley Kubrick
Running Time: 152 minutes
(Black & White)
Released: 14th June 1962

1962 **THE DOCK BRIEF (1962)**
Sellers as Morgenhall
With: Richard Attenborough, Beryl Reid, Frank Pettingell and David Lodge
Screenplay by John Mortimer and Pierre Rouve
Based on the play by John Mortimer
Directed by James Hill
Running Time: 88 minutes
(Black & White)
Released: 1st September 1962

General Leo Fitzjohn on his mount in *The Waltz of the Toreadors*.

1963 **THE WRONG ARM OF THE LAW**

Sellers as Pearly Gates

With: Lionel Jeffries, Bernard Cribbins, Davy Kaye, Nanette Newman, Bill Kerr, Graham Stark and John Le Mesurier
Screenplay by Len Heath and John Warren
Story by Ray Galton, Alan Simpson and John Antrobus
Directed by Cliff Owen
Running Time: 94 minutes (Black & White)
Released: 14th March 1963

1963 **HEAVENS ABOVE!**

Sellers as The Reverend John Smallwood

With: Isabel Jeans, Cecil Parker, Brock Peters, Ian Carmichael, Irene Handl, Eric Sykes and Bernard Miles
Screenplay by Frank Harvey and John Boulting
Directed by John Boulting
(Produced by Roy Boulting)
Running Time: 118 minutes (Black & White)
Released: 21st May 1963

THE PINK PANTHER

Sellers as Inspector Jacques Clouseau

With: David Niven, Robert Wagner, Capucine, Claudia Cardinale, Brenda de Banzie and Colin Gordon

Screenplay by Maurice Richlin and Blake Edwards
Directed by Blake Edwards
Running Time: 113 minutes (Colour)
Released: 9th January 1964

1964 DOCTOR STRANGELOVE, OR HOW I LEARNED TO STOP WORRYING AND LOVE THE BOMB

Sellers as Captain Lionel Mandrake, President Merkin Muffley and Doctor Strangelove

With: George C. Scott, Sterling Hayden, Keenan Wynn, Slim Pickens, Peter Bull, Tracy Reed and James Earl Jones
Screenplay by Stanley Kubrick, Terry Southern and Peter George
Based on the novel by Peter George – *Red Alert*
Directed by Stanley Kubrick
Running Time: 93 minutes (Black & White)
Released: 30th January 1964

Sellers' first screen appearance as Clouseau was in *The Pink Panther* which also starred David Niven and Capucine.

Sellers as President Merkin Muffley, one of his three roles in Stanley Kubrik's *Doctor Strangelove*.

Psychotic Viennese psychiatrist Doctor Fritz Fassbender has more problems than patients in *What's New, Pussycat?*

1964 THE WORLD OF HENRY ORIENT

Sellers as Henry Orient

With: Tippy Walker, Merri Spaeth, Angela Lansbury, Paula Prentiss, Phyllis Thaxter and Tom Bosley
Screenplay by Nora and Nunnally Johnson
Based on the novel by Nora Johnson
Directed by George Roy Hill
Running Time: 106 minutes (Colour)
Released: 20th March 1964

1964 A SHOT IN THE DARK

Sellers as Inspector Jacques Clouseau

With: George Sanders, Elke Sommer, Herbert Lom, Tracy Reed, Graham Stark and Burt Kwouk
Screenplay by Blake Edwards and William Peter Blatty
Directed by Blake Edwards
Running Time: 101 minutes (Colour)
Released: 20th June 1964

1965 WHAT'S NEW, PUSSYCAT?

Sellers as Doctor Fritz Fassbender

With: Peter O'Toole, Woody Allen, Romy Schneider, Ursula Andress, Paula Prentiss and Capucine
Screenplay by Woody Allen
Directed by Clive Donner
Running Time: 108 minutes (Colour)
Released: 23rd June 1965

1966 AFTER THE FOX

Sellers as Aldo Vanucci

With: Victor Mature, Britt Ekland, Lilia Brazzi, Akim Tamiroff, Martin Balsam and

Master criminal Aldo Vanucci, a.k.a. The Fox, in consultation with his mother.

Paola Stoppa
Screenplay by Neil Simon and Cesare Zavattini
Directed by Vittorio de Sicca
Running Time: 103 minutes (Colour)
Released: 29th September 1966

1967 CASINO ROYALE

Sellers as Evelyn Tremble

With: David Niven, Orson Welles, Ursula Andress, Deborah Kerr, Woody Allen, William Holden, Charles Boyer, John Huston and Peter O'Toole
Screenplay by Wolf Mankowitz, John Law and Michael Sayers
Uncredited additional script material by Terry Southern, Billy Wilder, Joe McGrath and Peter Sellers
Directed by Joe McGrath, Ken Hughes, Robert Parrish, Val Guest and John Huston
Running Time: 130 minutes (Colour)
Released: 14th April 1967

Spoof Bond adventure *Casino Royale*, featured real Bond girl, Ursula Andress.

1967 THE BOBO

Sellers as Juan Bautista

With: Britt Ekland, Rossano Brazzi, Adolfo Celi, Hattie Jacques, Ferdy Mayne, Kenneth Griffiths and John Welles
Screenplay by David R. Schwarz, from his play
Based on the novel by Burt Cole - *Olimpia*
Directed by Robert Parrish
Running Time: 105 minutes (Colour)
Released: 11th August 1967

Juan Bautista woos local beauty Olimpia, played by Sellers' wife, Britt Ekland, in *The Bobo*.

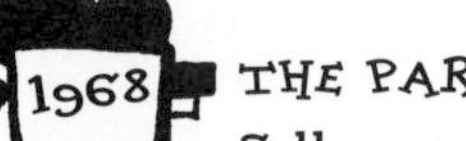

1968 THE PARTY

Sellers as Hrundi V. Bakshi

With: Claudine Longet, Marge Champion, Fay McKenzie, Steve Franken and Buddy Lester
Screenplay by Blake Edwards and Tom & Frank Waldman
Directed by Blake Edwards
Running Time: 98 minutes (Colour)
Released: 5th April 1968

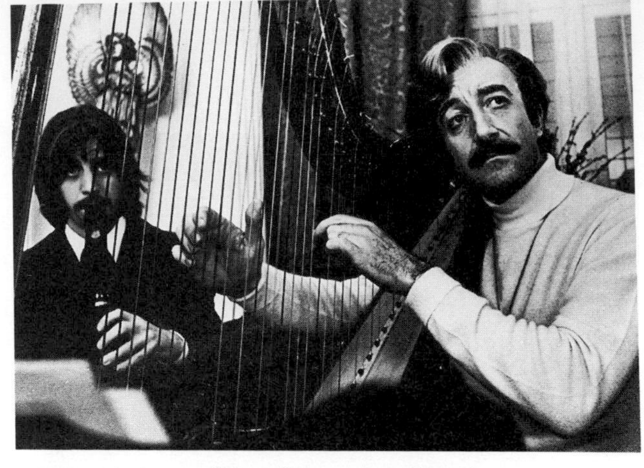

Eccentric multi-millionaire Sir Guy Grand in *The Magic Christian*.

1968 I LOVE YOU, ALICE B. TOKLAS

Sellers as Harold Fine

With: Jo Van Fleet, Joyce Van Patten, Leigh Taylor-Young, David Arkin and Herb Edelman
Screenplay by Paul Mazursky and Larry Tucker
Directed by Hy Averback
Running Time: 93 minutes (Colour)
Released: 8th October 1968

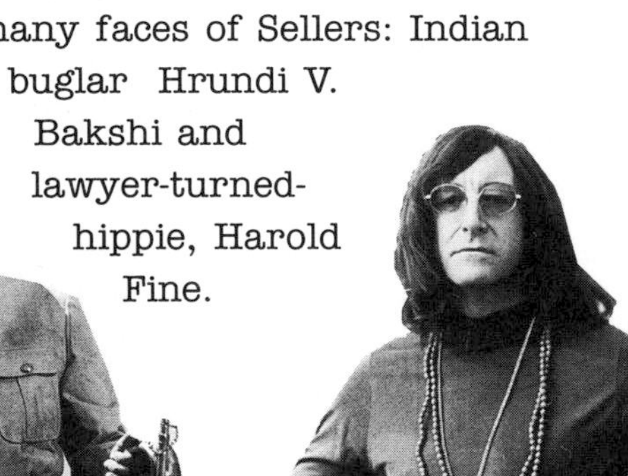

The many faces of Sellers: Indian bugler Hrundi V. Bakshi and lawyer-turned-hippie, Harold Fine.

1970 THE MAGIC CHRISTIAN

Sellers as Sir Guy Grand

With: Ringo Starr, Richard Attenborough, Laurence Harvey, Christopher Lee, Spike Milligan, Yul Brynner, Roman Polanski, Raquel Welsh, John Cleese, Wilfrid Hyde-White and John Le Mesurier
Screenplay by Terry Southern and Joe McGrath
Additional material by John Cleese, Graham Chapman and Peter Sellers
Based on the novel by Terry Southern
Directed by Joe McGrath
Running Time: 95 minutes (Colour)
Released: 12th February 1970

1970 HOFFMAN

Sellers as Benjamin Hoffman

With: Sinead Cusack, Jeremy Bulloch and Ruth Dunning
Screenplay by Ernest Gebler, based on his play
Directed by Alvin Rakoff
Running Time: 113 minutes (Colour)
Released: 16th July 1970

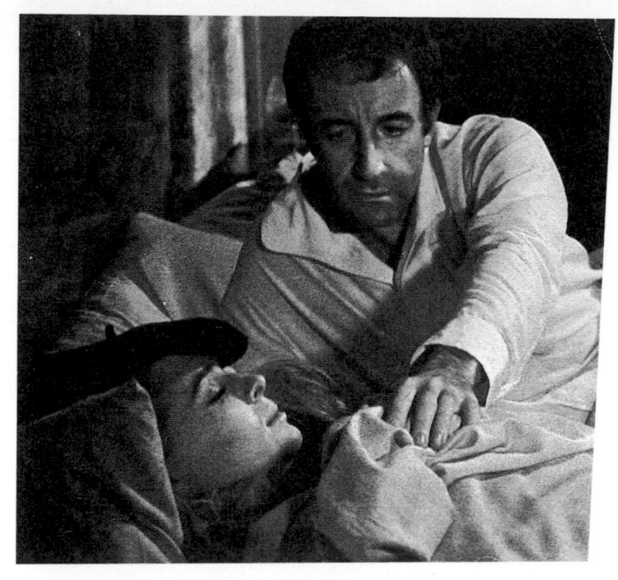

Sellers and Sinead Cusack co-starred in *Hoffman.*

1972 **WHERE DOES IT HURT?**
Sellers as Albert Hopfnagel
With: Jo Ann Pflug, Rick Lenz, Harold Gould, Eve Druce and Pat Morita
Screenplay by Rod Amateau and Budd Robinson
Based on their novel - *The Operator*
Directed by Rod Amateau
Running Time: 88 minutes (Colour)
Released: 11th August 1972

1970 **THERE'S A GIRL IN MY SOUP**
Sellers as Robert Danvers
With: Goldie Hawn, Tony Britton, Nicky Henson, John Comer, Judy Campbell and Diana Dors
Screenplay by Terence Frisby, from his play
Directed by Roy Boulting
(Produced by John Boulting)
Running Time: 96 minutes (Colour)
Released: 23rd November 1970

1970 **A DAY AT THE BEACH**
Sellers as The Salesman
With: Mark Burns, Beatrice Edney, Jack MacGowran, Fiona Lewis, Jorgen Kiil and Graham Stark
Screenplay by Roman Polanski
Based on a short story by Heere Heresma
Directed by Roman Polanski
Running Time: 88 minutes (Colour)
Released: (Unreleased)

Suave TV personality and professional lothario Robert Danvers meets his match in *There's A Girl in My Soup.*

1972 ALICE'S ADVENTURES IN WONDERLAND

Sellers as The March Hare

With: Fiona Fullerton, Michael Crawford, Robert Helpmann, Dudley Moore, Spike Milligan, Dennis Price, Flora Robson, Rodney Bewes, Peter Bull, Michael Horden and Ralph Richardson

Screenplay by William Sterling

Based on the novels by Lewis Carroll - *Alice in Wonderland* and *Alice Through The Looking Glass*

Directed by William Sterling

Running Time: 101 minutes (Colour)

Released: 7th December 1972

1973 THE BLOCKHOUSE

Sellers as Rouquet

With: Charles Aznavour, Jeremy Kemp, Per Oscarsson, Peter Vaughan, Nicholas Jones and Leon Lissek

Screenplay by John Gould and Clive Rees

Based on the novel by Jean-Paul Clebert

Directed by Clive Rees

Running Time: 88 minutes (Colour)

Released: (Unreleased)

1974 SOFT BEDS, HARD BATTLES

Sellers as General Latour, Major Robinson, Herr Schroeder, Prince Kyoto, the Narrator and Adolf Hitler

With: Lila Kedrova, Curt Jurgens, Gabriella Licudi, Jenny Hanley and Rula Lenska

Changing roles in *Soft Beds, Hard Battles.*

Screenplay by Leo Marks and Roy Boulting

Directed by Roy Boulting

(Produced by John Boulting)

Running Time: 107 minutes (Colour)

Released: 24th February 1974

1974 THE OPTIMISTS OF NINE ELMS

Sellers as Sam

With: Donna Mullane, John Chaffey, David Daker and Marjorie Yates

Screenplay by Anthony Simmons, from his novel

Directed by Anthony Simmons

Running Time: 110 minutes (Colour)

Released: 25th April 1974

Eccentric old busker Sam and his scruffy performing dog in *The Optimists of Nine Elms.*

1974

GHOST IN THE NOONDAY SUN

Sellers as Dick Scratcher

With: Anthony Franciosa, Spike Milligan, Clive Revill, Rosemary Leach and Peter Boyle
Screenplay by Evan Jones
Additional material by Spike Milligan
Based on the novel by Sid Fleischman
Directed by Peter Medak
Running Time: 89 minutes (Colour/Black & White)
Released: (Unreleased)
(Issued on video during the later 1980s)

1975

THE GREAT McGONAGALL

Sellers as Queen Victoria

With: Spike Milligan, Julia Foster, Julian Chagrin, John Bluthal, Valentine Dyall and Victor Spinetti
Screenplay by Spike Milligan and Joe McGrath
Inspired by the poems of William McGonagall
Directed by Joe McGrath
Running Time: 89 minutes (Colour)
Released: 23rd January 1975

1975

THE RETURN OF THE PINK PANTHER

Sellers as Inspector Jacques Clouseau

With: Christopher Plummer, Herbert Lom, Catherine Schell, Burt Kwouk, David Lodge and Graham Stark
Screenplay by Blake Edwards and Frank Waldman
Directed by Blake Edwards
Running Time: 113 minutes (Colour)
Released: 22nd May 1975

From Dick Scratcher in 1974 to Queen Victoria in 1975.

1976 THE PINK PANTHER STRIKES AGAIN

Sellers as Chief Inspector Jacques Clouseau

With: Herbert Lom, Colin Blakely, Leonard Rossiter, Lesley-Anne Down, Burt Kwouk and Omar Sharif

Screenplay by Blake Edwards and Frank Waldman

Directed by Blake Edwards

Running Time: 103 minutes (Colour)

Released: 16th December 1976

1976 MURDER BY DEATH

Sellers as Sidney Wang

With: David Niven, Maggie Smith, Peter Falk, James Coco, Elsa Lanchester, Alec Guinness, Nancy Walker, Estelle Winwood, James Cromwell and Truman Capote

Screenplay by Neil Simon

Directed by Robert Moore

Running Time: 94 minutes (Colour)

Released: 24th June 1976

Chief Inspector Jacques Clouseau is the master of inscrutable disguise.

REVENGE OF THE PINK PANTHER

Sellers as Chief Inspector Jacques Clouseau

With: Herbert Lom, Robert Webber, Dyan Cannon, Burt Kwouk, Paul Stewart, Robert Loggia and Graham Stark
Screenplay by Blake Edwards, Frank Waldman & Ron Clarke
Directed by Blake Edwards
Running Time: 98 minutes (Colour)
Released: 13th July 1978

Sellers with his actress wife Lynne Frederick on the set of *The Prisoner of Zenda*.

THE PRISONER OF ZENDA

Sellers as Syd Frewin and Prince Rudolph

With: Jeremy Kemp, Lynne Frederick, Lionel Jeffries, Gregory Sierra, Elke Sommer and Simon Williams
Screenplay by Dick Clement and Ian La Frenais
Based on the novel by Anthony Hope
Directed by Ricahrd Quine
Running Time: 108 minutes (Colour)
Released: 23rd May 1979

Chance, the gardener, who rises accidentally to political power in *Being There*.

BEING THERE

Sellers as Chance the Gardener

With: Shirley Maclaine, Melvyn Douglas, Jack Warden, Richard Dysart and Ruth Attaway
Screenplay by Jerzy Kosinski, from his novel
Directed by Hal Ashby
Running Time: 130 minutes (Colour)
Released: 19th December 1979

Sellers in his last film, *The Fiendish Plot of Dr. Fu Manchu.*

1980 THE FIENDISH PLOT OF DR. FU MANCHU (1980) (Posthumous Release)

Sellers as Nayland Smith and Dr. Fred Fu Manchu
With: David Tomlinson, Helen Mirren, Sid Caeser, Steve Franken, Simon Williams, Clive Dunn, Stratford Johns and John Le Mesurier
Screenplay by Jim Moloney and Rudy Dochtermann
Uncredited additional material by Peter Sellers
Directed by Piers Haggard
Uncredited additional sequences by Peter Sellers
Running Time: 104 minutes (Colour)
Released: 13th August 1980

1982 TRAIL OF THE PINK PANTHER (Posthumous Release)

Sellers as Chief Inspector Jacques Clouseau
Sellers features in unused sequences drawn from -THE PINK PANTHER STRIKES AGAIN and REVENGE OF THE PINK PANTHER

Other previously released scenes with Sellers are drawn from -THE PINK PANTHER, A SHOT IN THE DARK and THE RETURN OF THE PINK PANTHER
With: Joanna Lumley, Richard Mulligan (And in both new linking material and old footage from previous Panthers and unused sequences) Herbert Lom, David Niven, Capucine, Robert Loggia, Harvey Korman, Burt Kwouk, Graham Stark, Leonard Rossiter, Peter Arne and Ronald Fraser
Screenplay - See entries for other Panther films for Sellers material
New linking material by Blake and Geoffrey Edwards
Directed by Blake Edwards
Running Time: 97 minutes (Colour)
Released: 17th July 1982

Inspector Clouseau once again on the *Trail of the Pink Panther.*

GUEST APPEARANCES

Noted In Order Of Theatrical Release

During the 1960s, Sellers made several brief guest appearances in films that are worth detailing. (Technically, **A DAY AT THE BEACH** should be noted in this section. Although a detailed synopsis has been published, and even though Sellers was only present on set for a few days, the actual extent of his contribution remains unknown due to the elusiveness of a complete print of the film. Therefore, it has been included in the main Feature Films section and remains Sellers' only 'Lost' mainstream release. Even though they were not distributed at the time of their completion, both **GHOST IN THE NOONDAY SUN** and **THE BLOCKHOUSE** have now been released on home video in the USA, with the latter having yet to reach UK shores).

1962 ROAD TO HONG KONG

Sellers as The Indian Doctor

With: Bob Hope, Bing Crosby, Joan Collins, Robert Morley, Felix Aylmer and Walter Gotell

Other Cameo Appearances: David Niven, Dean Martin, Frank Sinatra, Jerry Colonna and Dorothy Lamour

Screenplay by Norman Panama and Melvin Frank

Directed by Melvin Frank

Running Time: 91 minutes (Black & White)

Released: May 22nd 1962

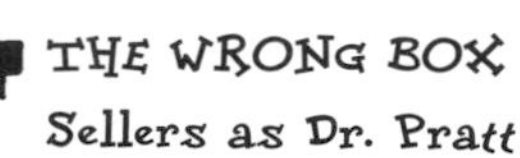

1966 THE WRONG BOX

Sellers as Dr. Pratt

With: Ralph Richardson, John Mills, Michael Caine, Wilfred Lawson, Nanette Newman, Peter Cook, Dudley Moore, Tony Hancock, Thorley Walters, Irene Handl and John Le Mesurier

Screenplay by Larry Gelbart and Robert Shevelove

Based on the novel by Robert Louis Stevenson

Directed by Bryan Forbes

Running Time: 110 minutes (Colour)

Released: 26th May 1966

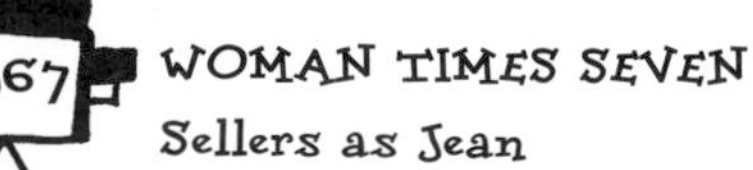

1967 WOMAN TIMES SEVEN

Sellers as Jean

With: Shirley Maclaine, Rossano Brazzi, Vittorio Gassman, Lex Barker, Michael Caine, Robert Morley, Alan Arkin and Patrick Wymark

Screenplay by Cesare Zavattini

Directed by Vittorio de Sica

Running Time: 99 minutes (Colour)

Released: 22nd June 1967

Sellers in traditional studio headgear.

FEATURE FILMS AND TV-MOVIE GUEST APPEARANCES

A CAROL FOR ANOTHER CHRISTMAS

Sellers and his then wife, Britt Ekland, filmed for three days, appearing as themselves, in this fund-raising spectacular for the United Nations. It does not appear to have been broadcast outside the USA.
Running time: 74 minutes (Colour)
Broadcast: 24th December 1964

FILM SHORTS & SUPPORT FEATURES

Noted In Production Order

Unless otherwise stated, all of the following were produced for theatrical release as second features. Where no information is available on the cast or production credits, the title of the subject has simply been listed alongside its year of release.

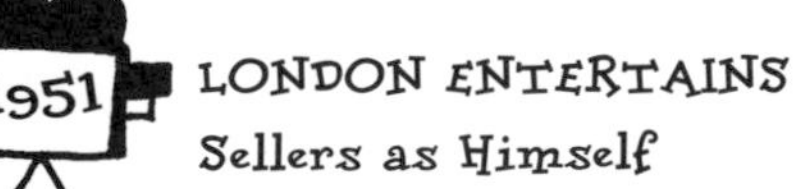

LONDON ENTERTAINS

Sellers as Himself
With: Eamon Andrews, Harry Secombe, Spike Milligan, Michael Bentine, Dennis Main Wilson, Christine Forrest, Pamela Bygraves, Vincent Ball, Diana Coupland and The Eastbourne Girls' Choir
Screenplay by Jimmy Grafton
Directed by E.J. Fancy
Running Time: 48 minutes
(Black & White)
Released: Circa August 1951

1951 LET'S GO CRAZY

Sellers as Groucho, Giuseppe, Cedric, Izzy Gozzunk & Crystal Jollibottom
With: Spike Milligan, Wallas Eaton, Manly & Austin and Freddie Mirfield's Garbage Men
Screenplay - Uncredited/Unknown
Directed by Alan Cullimore
Running Time: 32 minutes (Black & White)
Released: Circa September/October 1951

1953 THE SUPER SECRET SERVICE

Sellers as A Sophisticated City Gent
With: Dick Emery, Grahm Stark & The Ray Ellington Quartet
Screenplay by Spike Milligan
Directed by Charles W. Green
Running Time: 26 minutes
(Black & White)
Released: Circa May 1953

1956 THE CASE OF THE MUKKINESE BATTLEHORN

Sellers as Inspector Quilt, Henry Crun and Assistant Chief Commissioner Sir Jervis Fruit
With: Spike Milligan, Dick Emery, Pamela Thomas, Bill Hepper, Wally Thomas and Gordon Phillot
Screenplay by Harry Booth, John Penington and Larry Stephens
Directed by Joseph Sterling
Running Time: 29 minutes
(Black & White)
Released: Circa January 1956

1957 **COLD COMFORT**
Sellers as Hector Dimwittie and The Narrator
With: Clarise Granger and Kathleen St. George
Screenplay by Lewis Greifer and Maurice Wiltshire
Directed by James Hill
Running Time: 17 minutes
(Black & White)
Released: Circa April/May 1957

1957 **INSOMNIA IS GOOD FOR YOU**
Sellers as Hector Dimwittie and The Narrator
With: Clarise Granger
Screenplay by Lewis Greifer and Maurice Wiltshire
Directed by James Hill
Running Time: 17 minutes (Black & White)
Released: Circa April/May 1957

DEARTH OF A SALESMAN
Sellers as Hector Dimwittie and The Narrator
With: Clarise Granger and Richard Wattis
Screenplay by Lewis Greifer and Maurice Wiltshire
Directed by James Hill
Running Time: 17 minutes (Black & White)
Released: Circa May/June 1957

THE RUNNING, JUMPING AND STANDING STILL FILM
Sellers as Tweed Suited Gamekeeper
With: Spike Milligan, Mario Fabrizi, Graham Stark, Johnny Vyvyan, Leo McKern, David Lodge, Joe McGrath and Richard Lester
Screenplay - Credited as Thoughts by Spike Milligan, Peter Sellers, Mario Fabrizi and Richard Lester
Directed by Richard Lester
Running Time: 11 minutes
(Black & White)
Released: Circa November/December 1959

CLIMB UP THE WALL
No Information Available

LIGHT OF DAY
No Information Available

SIMON, SIMON
Sellers as Himself
Cameo Appearance
With: Graham Stark, Julia Foster, Norman Rossington, Paul Whitsun Jones, Audrey Nicholson, Kenneth Earle and Tommy Godfrey
Other Cameo Appearances: Michael Caine, Pete Murray, Eric Morecambe, Ernie Wise, David Hemmings, Bob Monkhouse and Bernie Winters
Screenplay by Graham Stark
Directed by Graham Stark
Running Time: 30 minutes (Colour)
Released: Circa Winter 1969

FILM SHORTS & SUPPORT FEATURES - Narration/Dubbing Credits

CHARLIE CHAPLIN'S 'BURLESQUE ON CARMEN' (1951)

Sellers as The Narrator

A re-release of Chaplin's 1915 short, which parodied the plot of Bizet's *Carmen*
Running Time: 17 minutes (Black & White)

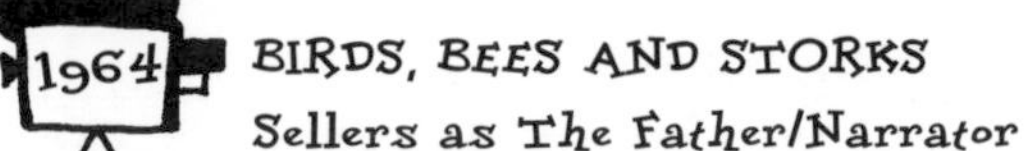

BIRDS, BEES AND STORKS

Sellers as The Father/Narrator

Based on the Story and Illustrations by Gerard Hoffnung
Directed by John Halas (A Halas & Batchelor Cartoon)
Running Time: 5 minutes (Colour)

THE GREAT PRAM RACE

Sellers as The Sports Commentator/Narrator

No Other Information Available

Between 1950-1956, Sellers was often called upon by Producers to re-dub dialogue or add extra character voices to films in post-production. The following list represents a selection of the titles that Sellers was known to have been involved with.

THE BLACK ROSE

Bandit's Voice

BEAT THE DEVIL

Humphrey Bogart's Voice

Due to a jaw injury, Bogart was unable to record certain lines

OUR GIRL FRIDAY

The Parrot's Voice

MALAGA

The Whole Cast

AKA - FIRE OVER AFRICA

THE MAN WHO NEVER WAS

Winston Churchill's Voice

Television Appearances

Television Series

Noted in order of Production

There are six main series that Sellers was involved with throughout the course of their run, with three of them being made in 1956 and one just using his voice. Episode titles are noted where applicable.

AND SO TO BENTLEY

1 Season/13 Episodes

Hosted by and Starring Dick Bentley
With: Peter Sellers, Rosemary Miller, Jill Day and Bill Fraser
Scripts by Frank Muir and Dennis Norden
Transmitted Live from Alexandra Palace
Produced by BBC Television
Broadcast from October - December 1954

Selling watches at the BBC.

THE IDIOT WEEKLY PRICE 2d

1 Season/6 Episodes

Sellers as The Editor of The Idiot Weekly
With: Kenneth Connor, Graham Stark, Valentine Dyall, Patti Lewis, Spike Milligan (Ep. 1 & 6 only), Eric Sykes (Ep. 1 only), June Whitfied (Ep. 1 only), and Max Geldray (Ep. 6 only)
Scripts by Associated London Scripts
Edited by Eric Sykes
Additional material by Spike Milligan
Directed by Richard Lester
For Associated Rediffusion Television
Broadcast 24th February – 23rd April 1956

A SHOW CALLED FRED

1 Season/5 Episodes

With: Spike Milligan, Valentine Dyall, Kenneth Connor, Graham Stark, Patti Lewis and Max Geldray
Scripts by Spike Milligan and John Antrobus
Directed by Richard Lester
For Associated Rediffusion Television
Broadcast 2nd – 30th May 1956

Sellers and Kenneth Connor in *Idiot Weekly – Price 2d.*

1957

YES, IT'S THE CATHODE RAY TUBE SHOW

1 Season/6 Episodes

With: Peter Sellers, Michael Bentine & David Nettheim
Scripts by Michael Bentine and David Nettheim
Directed by Kenneth Carter
For Associated Rediffusion Television
Broadcast 11th February – 18th March 1957

Eccentric millinery is worn for 'Idiots Mail Bag', featured in the first programme of the TV series, *A Show Called Fred.*

SON OF FRED

1 Season/8 Episodes

With: Peter Sellers, Spike Milligan, Valentine Dyall, Kenneth Connor, Graham Stark, Patti Lewis, Max Geldray, John Vyvyan, Cuthbert Harding (Ep. 1-7 only), Mario Fabrizi (Ep. 3-8 only), Jennifer Lautrec (Ep. 3-5 only), The Alberts (Ep. 4-8 only) & Eric Sykes (Ep. 5 only)
Scripts by Spike Milligan and John Antrobus
Directed by Richard Lester
For Associated Rediffusion Television
Broadcast 17th September – 5th November 1956

Michael Bentine, David Nettheim and Sellers compose themselves before recording *Yes, It's the Cathode Ray Tube Show.*

THE TELEGOONS
2 Seasons/11 and 15 Episodes
With the voices of Peter Sellers, Harry Secombe and Spike Milligan
Scripts by Maurice Wiltshire
Based on the original radio scripts by Spike Milligan and Larry Stephens
Directed by Tony Young
For broadcast by BBC Television

SEASON ONE:
1: The Ascent of Mount Everest
2: The Lost Colony
3: The Fear Of Wages
4: Napoleon's Piano
5: The Last Tram
6: China Story
7: The Canal
9: The Hastings Flyer
10: The Mystery Of the Marie Celeste - Solved!
11: The International Christmas Pudding
8: The Choking Horror
(Postponed from its original broadcast slot)
Broadcast 10th October – 28th December 1963

SEASON TWO:
1: Scradje
2: The Booted Gorilla
3: The Underwater Mountain
4: The Dreaded Battered Pudding Hurler Of Bexhill-On-Sea
5: Tales Of Old Dartmoor
6: Lurgi Strikes Britain
7: Captain Seagoon R.N.
8: The First Albert Memorial To The Moon
9: The Whistling Spy Enigma
10: Tales Of MontMatre
11: The Africa Ship Canal
12: The Affair Of The Lone Banana
14: The Nadger Plague
15: The Siege of Fort Knight
13:The Terrible Revenge Of Fred Fu Manchu
(Postponed from it's original broadcast slot)
Broadcast 28th March – 1st August 1964

The Goons reunited for *The Telegoons* in 1963.

GUEST APPEARANCES

Noted In Order Of Broadcast

The following list comprises a selection of the key appearances that Sellers made in everything from variety shows to sitcoms. Such things as chat shows and general interviews are noted when they are of particular interest.

1948 NEW TO YOU (BBC TV)

Sellers appeared twice, performing variations of his stage routine of the time.

1952 TOP HAT RENDEZVOUS (BBC TV)

Sellers appeared in this weekly variety series towards the end of January, when he appeared in a sketch as an elderly actor recalling all of the famous stars he's worked with via a series of impersonations.

An early cookery programme.

TRIAL GALLOP (BBC TV)

Unbroadcast

Sellers and Bentine were due to appear in this early attempt to transfer the humour of The Goon Show to the small screen. It was due to be shown on 13th February, but was cancelled due to the death of King George VI.

GOONREEL - A TELEVISION NEWS REEL (BBC TV)

Sellers, Milligan and Bentine were present at the Alexandra Palace Studios, while Secombe participated via filmed inserts. Scripted by Bentine, Milligan and Jimmy Grafton, it was broadcast on 2nd July.

DON'T SPARE THE HORSES (BBC TV)

A variety show broadcast live from the Princess Theatre in London, Milligan and Sellers featured in several sketches penned by Jimmy Grafton. Some unconfirmed evidence suggests that Sellers did a routine impersonating Groucho Marx at one point. It was screened on 1st November.

ALFRED MARKS TIME (BBC TV) Sellers appeared in a sketch disguised as his old gang show boss, Ralph Reader. It was such an accurate imitation that many viewers became convinced that they were watching the real thing.

SECOMBE HERE! (BBC TV) Sellers appeared in the third and final episode of Secombe's variety series, which went out live from the Earl's Court Radio Show on 3rd September.

THE CHRYSLER SHOW (CBS TV) Sellers flew to Canada during the last week of November to make his first non-UK television appearance, which involved him parodying Olivier's rendition of RICHARD III.

OFF THE RECORD (BBC TV) Sellers and Milligan appeared together to mime to the recently released Goon single, 'The Ying Tong Song'. The show was hosted by Jack Payne and broadcast on 12th December.

SALUTE TO SHOW BUSINESS (ITV) Sellers co-hosted this variety spectacular and also appeared as a ship's bar man, who seemed to be a not too distant cousin of Amphibulos from **CARLTON BROWNE OF THE F.O.** The programme was screened on 20th September.

THE BILLY COTTON BAND SHOW (BBC TV) During the late 1950s, Sellers made several guest appearances in the popular variety shows of the time, which apart from this one included **THE SIX FIVE SPECIAL (1958)** and **THE DICKIE VALENTINE SHOW (1958)**. He also worked on a one-off comedy special for the BBC called **THE APRIL 8TH SHOW (1958)**, with the joke being that it was shown on 1st April.

Sellers in *Top Hat Rendezvous*.

1958 THIS IS YOUR LIFE (BBC TV)

Sellers, along with Milligan and Ray Ellington, made a surprise appearance at the end of the show dealing with Harry Secombe's life story during the winter of 1958. Additionally, Sellers is known to have been on the show on at least two other occasions; firstly, when Kenneth More was its subject in 1960, and secondly, when it was Milligan's turn in 1973 with Sellers walking on disguised as a Nazi, complete with trench coat and tin helmet.

1959 THE ARTHUR PLOUGHSHARE SHOW (BBC TV)

Sellers appeared as a character called Pules Nogburt in an episode of this Eric Sykes penned series, which he also starred in.

TEMPO (ABC Television)

One of the early examples of Sellers' fascination with the poetry of William McGonagall, as he appeared as himself in this popular arts programme reading extracts of his work from a lectern. The sequences featuring Sellers were Directed by Joe McGrath.

THE STEVE ALLEN SHOW USA

The day before he suffered his first heart attack, Sellers appeared on this long-running talk show and after a brief chat with Allen, he took up his host's offer to join him and the programme's orchestra for a jam session. It's one of the few instances where Sellers' skill as a drummer was seen on screen. The programme went out live on 5th April.

NOT ONLY, BUT ALSO... (BBC TV)

Shortly into the run of the first season of Peter Cook and Dudley Moore's groundbreaking comedy show, Sellers asked Producer Joe McGrath to let him make a guest appearance. He appeared in two sketches, in one as a boxer and in the other as a critic. The resulting programme achieved what Sellers wanted, and proved to the public that he could still work after surviving his heart attack.

As myopic pugilist in *Not Only, But Also. . .*

1965 THE MUSIC OF LENNON AND McCARTNEY (Granada Television)

Sellers appeared in full costume as Richard III to perform his recently released cover version of 'It's Been A Hard Day's Night'. The segment in question was pre-recorded and mixed in with other footage of The Beatles performing in front of the cameras. It was screened during Christmas that year.

1966 THE BRADEN BEAT (BBC TV)

Sellers appeared on this popular magazine programme, hosted by Bernard Braden, as the celebrity reader for the viewers' letters that week. It was screened circa March/April.

SECOMBE & FRIENDS (Associated Rediffusion)

Sellers, Secombe and Milligan were reunited with the Ray Ellington Quartet to perform a Goon Show script in front of a live studio audience for the first time in six years. Extracts of 'The Whistling Spy Enigma' were intercut with interviews with Secombe and Ellington in the finished programme, which was broadcast on 16th October. A complete recording of the whole Goon Show performance is known to have survived intact.

Sellers played the King of Hearts in the BBC's *Alice's Adventures in Wonderland.*

1966 ALICE'S ADVENTURES IN WONDERLAND (BBC TV)

Jonathan Miller adapted and directed this version of Lewis Carroll's classic story, with Sellers as the King Of Hearts alongside Flora Robson as his Queen. The rest of the all-star cast included Sir John Gielgud, Sir Ralph Richardson, Sir Michael Redgrave, Malcolm Muggeridge, Peter Cook, Leo McKern and Wilfred Bramble. Anne Marie Malik played Alice, and the resulting 80-minute play was broadcast over Christmas that year.

1967 THE HEART OF SHOW BUSINESS (ATV)

Sellers, Secombe and Milligan joined forces as The Goons to appear in this variety show which was staged to raise funds for the Aberfan Disaster Charity. They revived their comedy strong-man act, The Three Charlies, from their touring days in a seven minute sketch, and the finished programme was screened on Easter Day.

1968 LAUGH IN (NBC)

Dan Rowan and Dick Martin's legendary American sketch show was into its second season when Sellers guest starred. He was filming **I LOVE YOU, ALICE B. TOKLAS** in the USA at the time.

1968 THE GOON SHOW – TALES OF MEN'S SHIRTS (Thames Television)

Another attempt at bringing The Goon Show to television, and this time in colour and with John Cleese as the announcer. Milligan slightly revised his original script and the show was produced by their old radio boss, Peter Eton, with Joe McGrath directing. The resulting 25-minute programme was broadcast on 8th August.

1969 FILM NIGHT (BBC TV)

Milligan and Sellers were filmed

Harry Secombe and Sellers join Parkinson for a special Goon edition of his chat show in 1972.

being interviewed on stage at the Roundhouse Theatre in London, during the production of **THE MAGIC CHRISTIAN**, and when questions were opened to the audience they were predominantly about The Goon Show.

WILL THE REAL PETER SELLERS (Stand Up)? (BBC TV)

Tony Palmer and his camera crew trailed after Sellers while **THE MAGIC CHRISTIAN** was being shot, and the resulting fly-on-the-wall documentary was something that Sellers fought to ban. The reason was quite simple; it painted him as a depressive and moody character, which was the last thing that the public and critics alike expected to see when it was shown in the winter.

PARKINSON MEETS THE GOONS (BBC TV)

Sellers and Secombe joined chat-show host Michael Parkinson in the studio, while the pneumonia ridden Milligan was seen on inserts filmed in Australia. The show was broadcast to publicise the upcoming TV version of **THE LAST GOON SHOW OF ALL** on 28th October, and it proved to be so popular with both its host and the public that it was screened shortly thereafter to close that particular season of the series.

1972 SYKES (BBC TV)

Sellers appeared as Little Tommy Grando, an escaped convict and old childhood friend of Eric Sykes and Hattie Jacques, who hides out in their house in an episode called 'Sykes...And A Stranger' which went out in early December.

THE LAST GOON SHOW OF ALL (BBC TV)

The TV recording of the show staged at the Camden Theatre on April 30th as part of the BBC's 50th Anniversary celebrations. Sellers, Secombe, Milligan, The Ray Ellington Quartet and Max Geldray were all present, and the programme was produced by John Browell and Directed for television by Joe McGrath. A highlight of the Christmas programming that year, it was shown on Boxing Day.

THE CAMPBELLS ARE COMING (ATV)

A variety special hosted by and starring Glen Campbell, with Sellers making a brief appearance as a gangster in a sketch alongside Omar Sharif. It was screened on 12th June.

PARKINSON (BBC TV)

A return appearance for Sellers on this popular chat show, with the whole programme being devoted to his reminiscences about his early days in variety to working on films. Several minutes of PANTHER outakes were also shown, with the programme being broadcast during the Autumn.

Omar Sharif and Sellers in *The Campbells are Coming.*

SING A SONG OF SECOMBE (BBC TV)

Sellers was reunited with Secombe and Milligan in two sketches for this Christmas Special, which was shown on 29th December. One saw them playing the notorious McGonagall Brothers and in the other, shot on location in Oxford Street in central London, they were seen in disguise as buskers playing to the passing crowds who completely failed to recognise them.

1975 **FACE YOUR IMAGE (BBC TV)**
A series where each week's celebrity guest had to sit and watch recordings of friends saying exactly what they thought about their character and personality, and then comment on how they felt about what had been said. Sellers was seen commenting from the set of **THE RETURN OF THE PINK PANTHER** on that weeks subject, Spike Milligan.

1976 **THE END OF THE PIER SHOW (BBC TV)**
A bizarre comedy special starring John Welles, John Bird and Percy Thrower. Sellers made an appearance as Adolf Hitler, who's later revealed to be an upper class cad with him clearly playing the part as Grytpype Thynne. Screened during July.

1978 **THE MUPPET SHOW (ATV)**
Variety show hosted by Kermit the Frog, courtesy of Jim Henson's puppetry, which Sellers guest starred in at the start of the programme's second season. After briefly being seen as Clouseau during the pre-title sequence, he was then on view in two musical numbers ('A Gypsy's Violin' and 'Cigarettes And Whisky') and a sketch as a German Physiotherapist. The show went out during the spring.

1978 **CLAPPERBOARD (ITV)**
Children's film magazine programme concentrating on behind-the-scenes and location reports, hosted by Chris Kelly. Sellers featured in one edition during the summer being interviewed by his trailer on the set of **REVENGE OF THE PINK PANTHER**, which was shown to tie in with the cinema release of the said film.

1980 **IT'LL BE ALRIGHT ON THE NIGHT (ITV)**
One of the earliest editions of Dennis Norden's annual programme of out-takes from film and TV had a pre-recorded interview with Sellers, as an introduction for the infamous 'Fart In The Lift' rushes from **REVENGE OF THE PINK PANTHER**, which was shot on the set of **THE FIENDISH PLOT OF DR. FU MANCHU**. Shown during Easter that year.

Sellers immerses himself in Muppet-style humour.

COMMERCIALS

During the mid-1950s, Sellers and Kenneth Conner joined forces to become the chimps' voices in the first six PG Tips tea adverts.

In 1973, during the shooting of GHOST IN THE NOONDAY SUN, an advert for Benson and Hedges Cigarettes, featuring Sellers, James Villiers and Milligan was shot for use in cinemas.

In 1975, Sellers shot a variety of adverts, again for use in cinemas, for TWA Airlines. Several different characters were used, including Thrifty McTravel, Jeremy 'Piggy' Peak Tyme and an Italian pop star called Vito.

In 1980, Sellers shot three adverts as Monte Casino, a Jewish con-man, for Barclaycard. A fourth TV advert was due to be shot, reuniting him with Irene Handl, but his ill-health brought filming to a stop after the third one had been completed.

RADIO APPEARANCES

RADIO SERIES

Sellers worked on several long running and short-lived series, which are listed in the second half of this sub-section. It is, however, worth going into some detail over what is perhaps one of the most famous radio shows ever produced...

THE GOON SHOW

Season One

Billed as 'CRAZY PEOPLE - Featuring Our Crazy Gang - The Goons' (17 episodes)

With: Peter Sellers, Harry Secombe, Spike Milligan, Michael Bentine,
The Ray Ellington Quartet, The Stargazers and Max Geldray
Announcer – Andrew Timothy (Ep. 1-7 and 11-17)
Denys Drower (Ep. 8-10)
Scripts by Spike Milligan and Larry Stephens
Edited by Jimmy Grafton
Produced by Dennis Main Wilson
Broadcast 28th May – 20th September 1951

CINDERELLA BBC Christmas Pantomime

With: Lizbeth Webb, Graham Stark, Peter Sellers, Harry Secombe, Spike Milligan, Michael Bentine, The Ray Ellington Quartet, The Stargazers and Max Geldray
Produced by Dennis Main Wilson
Broadcast 26th December 1951

Season Two

Billed as THE GOON SHOW from this point onwards (25 Episodes)

With: Peter Sellers, Harry Secombe, Spike Milligan, Michael Bentine,
The Ray Ellington Quartet, The Stargazers (Ep. 1-6 only) and Max Geldray
Scripts by Spike Milligan and Larry Stephens
Edited by Jimmy Grafton
Produced by Dennis Main Wilson
Broadcast 22nd January - 15th July 1952

Season Three (25 Episodes)

With: Peter Sellers, Harry Secombe, Spike Milligan (Ep. 1-4 and 17-25),
The Ray Ellington Quartet, Max Geldray,
Dick Emery (Ep. 7, 9, 11, 13, 15 and 17),
Graham Stark (Ep. 10, 12, 14 and 16),
Valentine Dyall (Ep. 14), Ellis Powell (Ep. 8) and Carol Carr (Ep. 7)
Announcer - Andrew Timothy
Scripts by Spike Milligan and Larry Stephens
Edited by Jimmy Grafton
Produced by Peter Eton (Ep. 1-17 and 20-25)
Charles Chilton (Ep. 18 and 19)
Broadcast 11th November 1952 - 5th May 1953
(Including Christmas Pantomime Episode Robin Hood, on 26th December 1952)

CORONATION EDITION
BBC Special

With: Peter Sellers, Harry Secombe, Spike Milligan, The Ray Ellington Quartet and Graham Stark
Script by Spike Milligan and Larry Stephens
Edited by Jimmy Grafton
Produced by Peter Eton
Broadcast 1st June

Season Four (30 Episodes)

With: Peter Sellers, Harry Secombe, Spike Milligan, The Ray Ellington Quartet and Max Geldray
Announcers - Andrew Timothy (Ep. 1-5), Wallace Greenslade (Ep. 6-30)
Scripts by Spike Milligan and Larry Stephens (Ep. 1-9 and 11-20), Larry Stephens (Ep. 10), Spike Milligan (Ep. 21-30)
Produced by Peter Eton (Ep. 1-14 and 16-30) Jacques Brown (Ep. 15)
Broadcast 2nd October 1953 - 19th April 1954

(* Insert recorded for CHRISTMAS CRACKERS broadcast on December 25th 1953)
(Michael Bentine returned for Ep. 13)

ARCHIE IN GOONLAND
BBC Special

With: Peter Brough and Archie Andrews, Peter Sellers, Harry Secombe, Spike Milligan & Hattie Jacques
Script by Eric Sykes and Spike Milligan
Produced by Roy Speer
Broadcast 11th June 1954

The Goons rehearsing in 1968 for a television adaptation of their radio series.

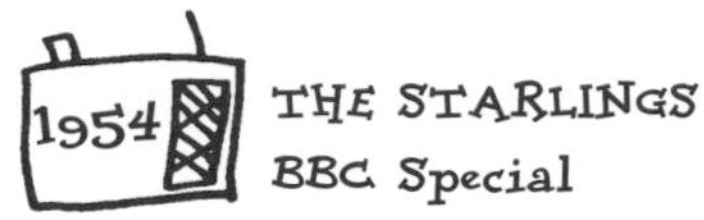

THE STARLINGS
BBC Special

With: Peter Sellers, Harry Secombe, Spike Milligan and Andrew Timothy
Script by Spike Milligan
Produced by Peter Eton
Broadcast 31st August 1954

Season Five (26 Episodes)

With: Peter Sellers, Harry Secombe, Spike Milligan, The Ray Ellington Quartet, Max Geldray, Valentine Dyall (Ep. 6 only), Charlotte Mitchell (Ep. 14 only) and John Snagge (Ep. 20)
Announcer - Wallace Greenslade
Scripts by Spike Milligan (Ep. 1-6), Spike Milligan and Eric Sykes (Ep. 7-26)
Produced by Peter Eton
Broadcast 28th September 1954 - 22nd March 1955

Season Six (27 Episodes)

With: Peter Sellers, Harry Secombe, Spike Milligan, The Ray Ellington Quartet, Max Geldray, Valentine Dyall (Ep. 20 only), Charlotte Mitchell (Ep. 18 only) and John Snagge (Ep 14, 23 & 26)
Announcer - Wallace Greenslade
Scripts by Spike Milligan (Ep. 3-17 and 19-24)
Spike Milligan and Eric Sykes (Ep. 1-2 and 18),
Spike Milligan and Larry Stephens (Ep. 25-27)
Produced by Peter Eton (Ep. 1-21),
Pat Dixon (Ep. 22-27)
Broadcast 20th September 1955 - 15th November 1955
(Ep. 10 postponed until 3rd April 1956)
29th November 1955 - 20th March 1956

Milligan shows his stripes.

The Missing Christmas Parcel - Post Early for Christmas, a special broadcast during **Children's Hour**, written by Eric Sykes and featuring Sellers, Secombe and Milligan was broadcast 8th December 1955

The Goons Hit Wales, a sketch by Milligan for St. David's Day was broadcast 1st March 1956, with Sellers, Secombe and Milligan all present for this 50 minute special

CHINA STORY
BBC Special

A remake of Ep. 17/Season Five recorded live at the National Radio Show
With: Peter Sellers, Harry Secombe, Spike Milligan, Ray Ellington and Max Geldray
Script by Spike Milligan and Eric Sykes
Produced by Dennis Main Wilson
Broadcast 29th August 1956

Season Seven (25 Episodes)
With: Peter Sellers, Harry Secombe, Spike Milligan (Ep. 1-3 and 5-25),
The Ray Ellington Quartet, Max Geldray, Valentine Dyall (Ep. 2 and 5),
George Chisholm (Ep. 4 and 15), Bernard Miles (Ep. 16) and Jack Train (Ep. 17)
Announcer - Wallace Greenslade
Scripts by Spike Milligan and Larry Stephens (Ep. 1, 3-22, and 24-25),
Spike Milligan (Ep. 2 and 23)
Produced by Peter Eton (Ep. 1-2),
Pat Dixon (Ep. 3-25)
Broadcast 4th October 1956 - 1st November 1956
(Ep. 5 postponed until 14th February 1957)
15th November 1956 - 28th March 1957
(Two special episodes were recorded for overseas transmission only during work on this season)

THE REASON WHY
BBC Special

With: Peter Sellers, Harry Secombe, Spike Milligan and Valentine Dyall
Announcer - Wallace Greenslade
Script by Spike Milligan
Produced by Jacques Brown
Broadcast 28th August 1957

Season Eight (26 Episodes)
With: Peter Sellers, Harry Secombe (Ep. 2-26), Spike Milligan,
The Ray Ellington Quartet (Ep. 1-12, 14-17 and 19-26), Max Geldray (1-7 and 9-26),
George Chisholm (Ep. 16, 18 and 23),
Dick Emery (Ep. 1 only),
Cecile Chevreau (Ep. 14 only), John Snagge (Ep. 24 only) and A.E. Matthews (Ep. 25 only)
Announcer - Wallace Greenslade
Scripts by Spike Milligan (Ep. 1, 16, 18, 20, 22, 24-25),
Spike Milligan and Larry Stephens (Ep. 2-10, 12-14 and 21),
Spike Milligan and John Antrobus (Ep. 23 and 26),
Larry Stephens and Maurice Wiltshire (Ep. 15, 17 and 19),
Larry Stephens (Ep. 11)
Produced by Charles Chilton (Ep. 1-5 and 17-26),
Roy Speer (Ep. 6 - 14),
Tom Ronald (Ep. 15 and 16)

A reunion at The Grafton, the London pub where the first Goon shows were hatched twenty-five years previously.

Broadcast 30th September 1957 - 24th March 1958

VINTAGE GOONS
14 Selected Remakes of Past Episodes

With: Peter Sellers, Harry Secombe, Spike Milligan, The Ray Ellington Quartet and Max Geldray
Announcer - Wallace Greenslade
Scripts by Spike Milligan
Produced by Charles Chilton (Ep. 1-2 and 9-14),
Roy Speer (Ep. 3-7),
Tom Ronald (Ep. 8 only)
Broadcast 6th October 1957 - 23rd March 1958
(Not broadcast on weekly basis.)

Season Nine (17 Episodes)
With: Peter Sellers (Ep. 1-10 and 12-17), Harry Secombe (Ep. 1-16), Spike Milligan, The Ray Ellington Quartet, Max Geldray, John Snagge (Ep. 10 and 11), Andrew Timothy (Ep. 14), George Chisholm (Ep. 15), Kenneth Conner (Ep. 11 and 17), and Valentine Dyall, Graham Stark and Jack Train (All Ep. 11)
Announcer - Wallace Greenslade
Scripts by Spike Milligan (Ep. 1-6 and 8-17)
Larry Stephens and Maurice Wiltshire (Ep. 7 only)
Produced by John Browell
Broadcast 3rd November 1958 - 23rd February 1959

Season Ten (6 Episodes)
With: Peter Sellers, Harry Secombe, Spike Milligan, The Ray Ellington Quartet, Max

Geldray, John Snagge (Ep. 3 and 6) and Valentine Dyall (Ep. 5 only)
Announcer - Wallace Greenslade
Scripts by Spike Milligan
Produced by John Browell
Broadcast 24th December 1959 - 28th January 1960

THE LAST GOON SHOW OF ALL

BBC Special

With: Peter Sellers, Harry Secombe, Spike Milligan, The Ray Ellington Quartet and Max Geldray
Announcer - Andrew Timothy
Script by Spike Milligan
Produced by John Browell
Broadcast 5th October 1972

Milligan and Sellers receive a silver disk for selling 70,000 copies of their record 'The Last Goon Show of All'.

Radio Broadcasts

What follows is a selection of Sellers' other radio work, including his other main series and several examples of his variety broadcasting. This list runs in alphabetical order, and the year of broadcast is included where it is known.

1954

ALL STAR BILL

Sellers read the story of Dick Whittington And His Cat as Olivier's Richard III.

ARTHUR ASKEY'S CHRISTMAS SHOW

Sellers was heard impersonating Dick Bentley.

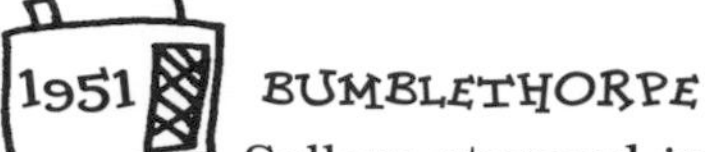

BUMBLETHORPE

Sellers stepped in at the last moment to replace Valentine Dyall for one episode in this series which starred Robert Moreton and Avril Angers, with Milligan in the supporting cast, who also worked on the script with Peter Ling and Larry Stephens.

1957 DESERT ISLAND DISCS

Sellers was Roy Plomley's guest on February 4th, and apart from his ten records his choice of book to be stranded with was *The Pickwick Papers* by Charles Dickens, and his one luxury item was a snorkel and a pair of flippers.

1956 FINKEL'S CAFE

Sellers was given a starring role in this sitcom dealing with the staff and customers of an Italian cafe in North London. A variety of star punters who passed through the establishment's doors included the likes of Katie Boyle and Sid James.

1964 FORCES GALA NIGHT

Sellers contributed to a Goons sketch, with Secombe and Milligan, via a landline from Paris, for this celebration of the 21st Anniversary of the British Forces Broadcasting Service in November that year.

1954 HAPPY HOLIDAY

An obscure series with Sellers featured in the supporting cast as the Mayor of a rundown seaside resort. Secombe guest starred in one of the eight episodes as a witless gangster.

19?? THE HUNDREDTH BOAT RACE

Jimmy Edwards and Dick Bentley starred in this one-off special which dealt with the people they encountered along the towpath during the said race. Three of the individuals they bumped into were Sellers, Secombe and Milligan. The show went out in April.

1955 THE LID OFF THE BBC

The fourth episode of this behind-the-scenes series looked at the making of The Goon Show, interviewing Sellers, Secombe and Milligan along the way. The show was broadcast during May.

Sellers and Avril Angers rehearse an episode of *Finkel's Café.*

1954 **THE LISTENING ROOM**
Sellers hosted an episode of this series and called upon a whole rosta of his characters from The Goon Show, with the odd moment of assistance from Milligan here and there, to introduce a selection of festive records with the programme going out on December 28th.

1949 **PETTICOAT LANE**
Another radio sitcom, this time with Sellers playing a variety of supporting characters, but mainly an East End spiv. Seven episodes were made in total.

1949 onwards **RAY'S A LAUGH**
Sellers joined Ted Ray's long running series from the very first episode, and his characters of Crystal Jollibottom and Guiseppe the Italian waiter became firm favourites with listeners. As the seasons progressed, film commitments and other radio work led to Sellers' appearances becoming more infrequent, but he certainly made the effort to take part whenever he could right up until the programme's last episode.

1950 **SELLERS MARKET**
Another star vehicle for Sellers, this time pairing him with Miriam Karlin as a pair of street market traders. The series lasted for eight episodes, and the title was later used for one of Sellers' albums.

1948 **THIRD DIVISION**
The first radio series to unite future Goons Harry Secombe, Michael Bentine and Sellers. Scripted by Frank Muir and Dennis Norden, the cast also included the likes of Benny Hill and Patricia Hayes. Six episodes were recorded in total.

Sellers is also known to have appeared in the following radio shows, dating from the late 1940s to the mid 1970s:

Calling All Forces
Caribbean Carnival
Curiouser And Curiouser
Paradise Street
Everything Under Control
Show Time
Stump The Storyteller
Tempo For Today
Worker's Playtime
Up And Coming
Henry Hall's Guest Night
Join In And Sing
It's Fine To Be Young
Northern Lights
Variety Bandbox
Woman's Hour
Open House
Top Of The Town
The Golden Slipper Club
Star Time

THEATRE APPEARANCES

As noted through the course of this book's main text, Sellers spent many years travelling around the variety hall circuit of England, Scotland and Wales, playing everywhere from the London Palladium to the Glasgow Empire. Any major points of interest from this period have been noted in earlier chapters.

Sellers' single experience on the West End Stage was in 1958 in a production called **BROUHAHA**, which opened at the Aldwych Theatre under Peter Hall's direction on August 27th that year, for a limited season. The cast included Leo McKern and the script was by George Tabori.

Pantomime proved to be an equally short-lived theatrical experience for Sellers, with **JACK AND THE BEANSTALK** being followed by and equally disasterous turn in **MOTHER GOOSE**, where his Colonel Bloodnok inspired character met with lukewarm applause at the end of every performance during the Christmas period of 1954.

Sellers also toured with The Goons, appearing at venues such as the Winter Gardens in Eastbourne and The Coventry Theatre where they played a six week season in The Birthday Show during October through to December 1955. Sellers' experiences as a child touring with his parents led him to avoiding performing on stage as an adult performer as often as he could.

From variety at the London Palladium in the 1940s to the West End stage in *Brouhaha.*

RECORDS

ALBUMS

Sellers released four comedy albums in total, all of which are now collectors' items and were re-released on CDs during the early 1990s.

THE BEST OF SELLERS

Originally released on Parlophone PMD 1069 1958
Produced by George Martin, the tracks run as follows:

1: 'The Trumpet Volunteer'
Written by Sellers/Hare
2: 'Auntie Rotter'
Written by Monkhouse/Goodwin
3: 'All The Things You Are'
Written by Kern/Hammerstein II
4: 'We Need The Money'
Written by Sellers/Hare
5: 'I'm So Ashamed'
Written by Hare
6: 'Party Political Speech'
Written by Max Schreiner
7: 'Balham - Gateway To The South'
Written by Muir/Norden/Goodwin
8: 'Suddenly It's Folk Song'
Written by Sellers/Fisher

SONGS FOR SWINGIN' SELLERS

Originally released on Parlophone PMC1111/PCS3003 1959
Produced by George Martin, the tracks run as follows:

1: 'You Keep Me Swingin'
Performed by Peter Sellers and Fred Flange (Matt Munro)
Written by Hare/Fisher
2: 'So Little Time'
Written by Muir/Norden
3: 'Lord Badminton's Memoirs'
Written by Schreiner/Goodwin
4: 'The Critics' (with Irene Handl)
Written by Schreiner/Goodwin
5: 'My Old Dutch'
Written by Ingle/Chevalier
6: 'Face To Face'
Written by Schreiner/Goodwin
7: 'In A Free State'
Written by Schreiner/Goodwin
8: 'Puttin' On The Smile'
Written by Sellers
9: 'Common Entrance'
Written by Muir/Norden
10: 'I Haven't Told Her, She Hasn't Told Me (But We Know It Just The Same)'
Written by Dubin/Kahal/Fain
11: 'Shadows On The Grass' (with Irene Handl)
Written by Handl
12: 'Wouldn't It Be Lovely'
Written by Lerner/Loewe
13: 'We'll Let You Know'
Written by Sellers
14: 'Peter Sellers Sings George Gershwin'
Written By Sellers

PETER AND SOPHIA

Originally released on Parlophone PMC1131/PCS3102 1960
Produced by George Martin, the tracks run as follows:

1: 'Goodness Gracious Me!' (with Sophia Loren)
Written by Lee/Kretzmer
2: 'Smith - An Interview With Sir Eric Goodness' (with Graham Stark)
Written by Bricusse
3: 'Zoo Be Zoo Be Zoo' (Loren solo)
Written by Shepherd/Tew
4: 'Ukelele Lady' (with The Temperance Seven)
Written by Kahn/Whiting
5: 'Setting Fire To The Policeman'
Written by Munro-Smith
6: 'Bangers And Mash' (with Sophia Loren)
Written by Lee/Kretzmer
7: 'Oh! Lady Be Good'
Written by Gershwin
8: 'To Keep My Love Alive' (Loren solo)
Written by Rodgers/Hart

No Sinatra – but swingin' nonetheless.

9: 'Why Worry?'
Written by Munro-Smith
10: 'Grandpa's Grave'
Written by dePaul/Gibson/Cavanaugh
11: 'I Fell In Love With An Englishman' (with Sophia Loren)
Written by Bricusse
12: 'Africa Today'
Written by Munro-Smith
13: 'Fare Thee Well' (with Sophia Loren)
Written by Fisher/Kretzmer

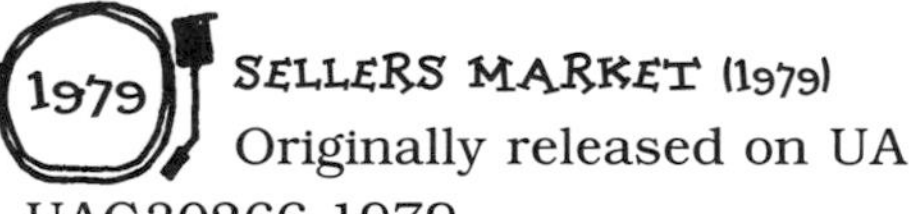

SELLERS MARKET (1979)
Originally released on UA UAG30266 1979
Produced by Ken Barnes, the tracks run

as follows:
The Musical Scene:
1: 'Night And Day'
Written by Porter
2: 'The All England George Formby Finals' Featuring:
- 'The Chinese Laundry Blues'
Written by Cotterall
- 'My Grandad's Flannelette Nightshirt'
Written by Formby/Latta
- 'Guarding The Home Of The Home Guard'
Written by Formby/Latta
- 'Hold Tight, Keep Your Seats, Please'
Written by Gifford/Cliffe/Formby
- 'They're Parking Camels Where The Taxis Used To Be'
Written by Grant/Rees
3: 'Gerfunk'
Written by Mercer
4: 'Singin' In The Rain'
Written by Freed/Brown
5: 'The Eaton Square Blues' (For Musicians Only)
Written by Clare/Crombie/Porter
6: Peter Sellers Sings Rudolph Friml Featuring: 'Only A Rose'
Written by Friml/Hooker
7: The Cultural Scene:
'The Complete Guide To Accents Of The British Isles'
Written by Moore/Kinton/Sellers/Barnes
Featuring: 'Don't Cry For Me Argentina'
Written by Rice/Lloyd-Webber
8: 'The Whispering Giant' (with Irene Handl)
Written by Handl

Albums Guest Appearances & Compilations

1961
BRIDGE ON THE RIVER WYE
With Secombe, Milligan & Peter Cook
Parlophone PMC 1131/PCS 3036

FOOL BRITANNIA
Ember CEL 902/EL31192

HOW TO WIN AN ELECTION (OR NOT LOSE BY MUCH) (1964)
With Secombe and Milligan
Philips AL 3464

HE'S INNOCENT OF WATERGATE (OR DICK'S LAST STAND)
With Milligan
Decca SKL 5194

COMMONERS CROWN - Steeleye Span
Sellers features on 'New York Girls'
Chrysalis CHR1071

1977
CAPTAIN BEAKY & HIS BAND
Sellers features on the tracks - 'The Haggis Season' and 'Jacques A Penniless French Mouse'
Polydor 2383462

THE PARKINSON INTERVIEW
(Edited highlights of 1974 Interview)
BBC REH 402

SONGS OF SELLERS
MFP 4156401

1990 THE PETER SELLERS COLLECTION
EMI ECC 5

1993 A CELEBRATION OF SELLERS
Sellers 1/7243 8 27781 2 7

Albums
Film & TV Tie-Ins

THE MUSIC, SONGS AND STORY OF TOM THUMB (1958)
MGM C 772

AFTER THE FOX (1966)
UA SULP 1151

THE BOBO (1967)
WB WS1711

THE MAGIC CHRISTIAN (1969)
Pye NSPL28133

ALICE'S ADVENTURES IN WONDERLAND (1972)
Warner Brothers K56009

THE OPTIMISTS (Of Nine Elms) (1973)
Paramount PAS1015

THE PINK PANTHER STRIKES AGAIN (1976)
UA UAS30176

REVENGE OF THE PINK PANTHER (1978)
UA UAS30012

THE MUPPET SHOW - VOLUME 2 (1978)
Pye NSPH 21

EPs

Three volumes of EPs were released from the material on THE BEST OF SELLERS, while four were made up from SONGS FOR SWINGIN' SELLERS and another three from PETER AND SOPHIA. All of them came out on the Parlophone label.

Material from the recordings of Peter Sellers and Peter Ustinov were put together to form an EP in 1962 called THE TWO PETERS. Although they were not heard together, a new Sellers track by the name of 'Fullers Earth' was included.

Sellers also featured on two EPs that were drawn from the FOOL BRITANNIA album in 1963, and in 1967 an EP simply entitled THE GOONS was issued by Decca.

78s & 45s

By Sellers

JAKKA AND THE FLYING SAUCERS (AN INTERPLANETARY TALE)
PARTS ONE & TWO (1953) (78)
DIPSO CALYPSO/NEVER NEVER LAND (1955) (78)
BOILED BANANAS AND CARROTS/ANY OLD IRON (1957) (78 & 45)
I'M SO ASHAMED/A DROP OF THE HARD STUFF (1958) (78 & 45)

PUTTIN' ON THE SMILE/MY OLD DUTCH (1959) (45)
GOODNESS GRACIOUS ME/GRANDPA'S GRAVE (1960) (45)
BANGERS AND MASH/ZOO BE ZOO BE ZOO (1960) (45)
A HARD DAY'S NIGHT/HELP (1965) (45)
AFTER THE FOX/THE FOX TROT (1966) (45)
THE HOUSE ON THE RUE SICHEL/MADAM GRENIERS THEME (1974) (45)
THANK HEAVEN FOR LITTLE GIRLS/SINGIN' IN THE RAIN (1978) (45)
THEY'RE PARKING CAMELS WHERE THE TAXIS USED TO BE/
NIGHT AND DAY (1979) (45)
THE UNRELEASED SHE LOVES YOU/
THE UNRELEASED SHE LOVES YOU b (1981) (45)
DANCE WITH ME HENRY/UNCHAINED MELODY (1990) (45)

By Sellers...With The Goons

THE BLUEBOTTLE BLUES/I'M WALKING BACKWARDS FOR CHRISTMAS
(1956) (78 & 45)
BLOODNOK'S ROCK N' ROLL CALL/THE YING TONG SONG (1956) (78 & 45)
I LOVE YOU/EEH! AH! OOH! (1957) (78 & 45)
A RUSSIAN LOVE SONG/WHISTLE YOUR CARES AWAY (1957) (78 & 45)
RHYMES/THE RASPBERRY SONG (1978) (45)

Goon Notes

Parlophone issued several volumes of Goon Show episodes as LPs under the titles of **THE BEST OF THE GOON SHOWS** (1959), **THE BEST OF THE GOON SHOWS - No. 2** (1960), **GOON...BUT NOT FORGOTTEN** (1967), **GOON AGAIN - GOON SHOWS** (1968) and **FIRST MEN ON THE GOON** (1971).

An album of songs by The Goons was compiled and released by Decca as **THE GOONS UNCHAINED MELODIES**.

The BBC released albums drawn from the soundtracks of the two **PARKINSON** shows Sellers featured on, with **MICHAEL PARKINSON MEETS THE GOONS**, and the previously mentioned solo Sellers album.

Since 1974, the BBC has been releasing The Goon Show on LPs, Tapes and more recently, CDs. The popularity of the material was proven to the company when they were awarded a silver disc for high sales figures when **THE LAST GOON SHOW OF ALL** LP hit the shops in 1972, and as of going to press, 14 volumes of the show have been released on double cassettes.

LAGRANGE
COGNAC

VARIETY CLUB OF
GREAT BRITAIN AWARD
TO
ALFIE BASS
I.T.V PERSONALITY
OF
1960